TIGER W
BIOGRAPHY

THE STORY OF GOLF LEGEND

Gilbert N Harroald

THE STORY OF GOLF LEGEND

TIGER WOODS

BIOGRAPHY

CONTENTS

INTRODUCTION

An fascinating writing and in-depth study of Tiger Woods' life and career as one of the greatest athletes of all time. This book immerses you in the remarkable narrative of a guy who faced severe adversity, fell into a crisis, and emerged with extraordinary energy and uncompromising tenacity.

Tiger Woods has become a global sports superstar, capturing the attention and adoration of millions around the world with his natural talent and excellent golfing ability. His life, however, was more than just grandeur and unwavering achievement. "Roaring Back" dives into Tiger Woods' journey, from peak achievements to unexpected problems and disappointments.

Tiger Woods enjoys golf and has won numerous titles and records, including 15 major championships. However, in 2009, his life was rocked by personal troubles and a controversy that threatened not just his job but also his honour and reputation. It's not surprising, then, that he didn't give up. Instead, he returned to the golf course with a strong will and a desire to reclaim his title.

This book not only examines Tiger Woods' enormous triumphs, but also the decline and rebirth of a person with the ability to overcome problems and recover from an unbelievable struggle. "Roaring Back" will provide you with an in-depth look into the fall and resurgence of a legend, as well as vital lessons on patience, hardship, and ascent.

Join us as we study Tiger Woods' terrible and spectacular journey, a man who demonstrated that a drop in energy and resilience may result in a rise and prosperity.

CHAPTER 1

THE HOGAN THING

Tiger Woods' fall and rise is defined by so many unique milestones that we must take the entire measure of Tiger's leap toward immortality at the 1997 Masters to compute the distance between zenith and nadir. So, before we look at his victory in 2019, examine his victory in the first one, twenty-two everlasting summers ago. That week in April in Augusta, Georgia seemed so tense and tense that it seemed surreal. For God's sake, tournament badges were selling for $8,000 and above. As a result of Tiger. Because he knew he was going to win.

But on that exhilarating week's cold Saturday morning, I was horrified to be attending a funeral for a friend of a new Augusta acquaintance. The day prior, Allen F. Caldwell III shot and killed himself. He'd worked as a ticket broker. In the blink of an eye, skyrocketing demand from corporate customers and unmet promises had wrecked him financially. That sad footnote tempered the joy of the week for a small number of individuals, which is a good thing, but I dwelled on it.

What on earth is going on? Despite the fact that the world and Tiger were clearly previously acquainted, using the race card in this first large commercial message seemed particularly callous. It wasn't a respectable method of selling clothes and shoes. And the notion that any course in the world would not spread out its red carpet for the rising worldwide celebrity was absurd.

Besides, Tiger seemed hesitant to accept the position of Ambassador of his Race, and who could blame him? He stated the only time he considered his ethnicity was when writers asked him about it, and he was adamant that he did not want to be labelled as black. Of course, race isn't only about melanin: Tiger grew up in a white community (2.7 percent of the 46,229 people in Cypress, CA, according to the 2000 census), played a white sport at a white high school, and had white friends and girlfriends. He wasn't black in the way that most white Americans consider black to be. Tired of answering queries that are truly none of your concern, remember Tiger's use of a portmanteau word to define his ethnic composition; he was Cablanasian, he stated, not Caucasian, black, or Asian. He embodied all three.

Mr. Woods and Mr. Sifford became friends because they had both experienced slights and racial injustice as young men. Earl was a decent baseball player in Kansas back in the day. He played catcher, a position reserved for the greatest athletes, and was the only person of colour on his youth all-star team, at the state youth tournament, at Kansas State, and across the Big 8 Conference. You've probably heard the story of how hotels refused to let him check in. Restaurants refused to serve him despite the fact that he was on the team. He would not be treated as an equal by inferior white people. In golf, Charlie is the same. At the age of seventeen, the ex-caddie from Charlotte turned pro and won the Negro National Open six times. But he couldn't establish himself—or earn a living—by winning the tournaments you read about in the media. So why not? There are three letters: PGA.

Although the Professional Golf Association of America had not admitted blacks or women since its formation in 1916, they legalised its racial discrimination in 1934 by placing the controversial "Caucasians only" rule into their by-laws. Presidents of the PGA of America during the twenty-seven years the whites-only rule was in effect, history is looking at you. Two in particular were significant in that they returned to Augusta: Ed Dudley was PGA president from 1942 to 1948. Big Ed, who won fifteen times on the PGA Tour, was also the pro at Augusta National since its inception in 1932 and for the next twenty-five years.

To some extent, cigar-chomping Charlie made up for lost time, but he was bitter and became even more so after winning a couple of regular tour tournaments but not being invited to play in the Masters. "These motherfuckers kept me out," he informed me in 1996. "Fuck Cliff Roberts"—Roberts, Jones's partner and co-founder of Augusta National and the Masters, who is also no longer alive. However, the reality was more convoluted than Charlie and his followers suggested. Several white golfers who had won a tour event in the past have also been denied a parking spot or a locker at Augusta National in April. Sifford, on the other hand, had been through a lot, and he told Tiger about it. A coaching change is a major issue for the virtuoso performers and high-maintenance perfectionists at the top of professional golf and tennis. Tiger's coach for the past seven super-successful years, John Anselmo, was fired. The helpful Huntington Beach-based pro's course, Meadowlark Golf Club, was only a thirty-minute drive from the Woods' home in Cypress. But Anselmo was getting older, unwell, and out of commission owing to colon cancer.

Aficionados looked for someone to compare to Tiger after his game-changing win in the 1997 Masters, and again in 2019. And the name God—that is, Hogan—kept popping up. Their similarities resided in their commitment to practise; the explosive strength of their swings—while keeping perfectly balanced; and their determination to work the ball high or low, left to right or right to left as the occasion dictated, regardless of the strain of the moment. Their small bodies' sheer athleticism. Their perseverance. Their coldness.

Hogan's horror began when four 300-pound lineman whose mothers never hugged them took off rushing and crashed into him with everything they had. Or, at least, that's how it seemed when the 346 cubic inch Cadillac monoblock flathead V-8 engine flew through the firewall of the car and into the body of the seated, helpless guy. Many bones broke at the same time—his pelvis, ribs, shoulder, and ankle—but a strong hit to the left side of his head, which punched his eye, thankfully did not break his skull. The accident happened on a cloudy morning in the Chihuahuan Desert on two-lane Highway 80 in west Texas in February 1949. The driver of a westbound

Greyhound bus, L.H. Hogan had foolishly passed the slow automobile in front of him. The bus weighed 20,000 pounds plus the weight of the people and their belongings, and it was travelling at roughly 35 miles per hour. Hogan's eastbound '48 Caddy was toast.

What Hogan did a split second before impact was critical to his safety as well as the tsunami of love and approval that was about to pour over him. When the bus's high headlights illuminated the interior of the car like lightning, Hogan yelled, "Look out!" and threw himself sideways in front of his wife, Valerie. Which comes first, bravery or instinct? Both, most likely. Diving hard to his right kept his wife safe and kept Ben from coming into violent contact with the steering column, which smashed into the car alongside the engine. The steering mechanism would have impaled him, as evidenced by the wreck after they'd taken him out of it.

"He saved my life," Valerie said, pale-faced, and she kept saying it. The phrase was repeated in the second or third paragraphs of hundreds of newspaper reports about the catastrophe the next day.

Hogan's image was altered at that moment. But only his image. Circumstances change, often very quickly, but whether people change is arguable. Who was this courageous man? Despite winning thirteen tournaments in 1946, seven in 1947, and ten in 1948, including the PGA Championship and the US Open, "Bantam Ben"—a nickname he despised—was a symbol of brilliance and a respected sports figure but not a household name, unlike Arnie and Tiger. This 145-pound battler with a 37-inch sleeve, the balance of a tightrope walker, a meticulous centre part, and the fast-twitch muscle fibres of a gunslinger was also tough as a two-dollar steak.

Six months before the catastrophe, one of the downs occurred. Hogan offered excellent offence in winning the Denver Open by sprinting off to catch a train to the next tournament while still having a chance to win this one. The leader, Fred Haas, Jr., collapsed at the finish line, and the absent Hawk triumphed. Dudgeon flew a mile high in Denver.

But that was before he nearly lost his own life saving his wife's.

Hundreds of letters to America's new hero came at the Hotel Dieu hospital, a huge redbrick facility in downtown El Paso. There were typically media around, documenting the ups and downs of his long rehabilitation, particularly his emergency operation for blood clots. He had been there for 59 days. He could see the winter sun set on the mountains of Mexico and hear the bells of St. Patrick Cathedral from his window. Photographers captured a terribly malnourished patient tied to a trolley at the train station on the day Mr. and Mrs. Hogan returned home. The man smiled bravely, while his wife looked tired and frightened.

He worked hard in rehab.

His comeback tournament, which sealed his fame and evoked Tiger at Augusta in 2019, took place a year and a half after the crash. Tiger was a prodigy who won six tournaments in his first fifteen months as a professional, including the 1997 Masters. But Tiger... After winning the 1997 Masters so handily, and then winning the GTE Byron Nelson Golf Classic and the Western Open a few weeks later, he concluded he disliked his swing. I despised it. He was not achieving the visual beauty he desired, according to videotape, and he was a little wild off the tee. No, he said to Butch, he didn't want incremental changes; he wanted a complete overhaul. He'd be ringing ancient adages in their ears: for Tiger, the question wasn't how many, but how well. He fixed it even though it wasn't broken. Tiger's other fallback was the time-honoured rhetorical strategy of people forced to speak when they have nothing to say: the cliché. Tiger could be counted on to communicate absolutely nothing before or after the competition, often rather ingeniously. Someone had presumably convinced Earl, who considered himself a brilliant media manipulator, that pens and microphones were the enemy, not a source of reliable free exposure. Hiding things from the press—hiding things from everyone—was part of his identity.

A number of other top golfers fought back from the brink of oblivion more than half a century ago. Their stories and the persons involved are nothing like Tiger's, except for their steadfast resolve to give up. Another thing that distinguishes all three is their obsessive quest of perfection (sorry, Lexus). If I may say so, I am highly opposed to both ideas. I am a big believer in giving up—on a poor career, a bad marriage, a horrible aim, whatever. Quitting is far more often the best option in life than sticking it out. Recognizing a lost cause or a lousy fit is a sign of discernment and adaptation in one's life, and it requires a higher level of intellect than "never give up."

And I reject the concept of perfection as an anchor on human activity. Done is the enemy of perfection. Perfect is the condemning voice reminding you that your physics grade could have been higher, that your form on your tour en l'air in Act II could have displayed more vigour and balance, that you shot 67 but missed two putts under eight feet, and that you shot 67 but missed two putts under eight feet. I say, screw it. Give it your all, get it done, and move on.

When the commencement speaker for a diesel truck repair school falls ill and they ask me to fill in, I intend to speak out strongly against determination and excellence. Grads, put that in your Juul and vape it. I'm expecting boos. The thing is, I simply don't understand champions who keep practising way past pretty damn excellent and who are never knocked off their course despite life's groyne kicks. If there's a decent bar in the hereafter, I'd like to discuss these topics with Tiger and a few others, such as Skip Alexander.

Stewart Murray "Skip" Alexander, a tall, pleasant Duke University student, could manage academics as well as a golf club. Skip, a North Carolina native from Durham, was hardly blue-blood; he'd learned the game as a caddie at a small country club. He mastered it to the point where he won the North Carolina Amateur and the North and South Amateurs at Pinehurst in 1941. The captain of the Blue Devils golf team graduated and then, like so many others, left for the next four and a half years, not returning home until the war was done.

He'd gone to the Pacific in general, and the Philippines in particular. He didn't say anything about it. The mustered-out vet was hired as an assistant at Lexington Golf Club, which is roughly twenty miles south of Winston-Salem. He mastered the time-honoured method of the golf pro who can't remember a hundred new names but has to act as if he cares about each and every member: he just named everyone "Pard" or "Dude." "How did you do today, Pard?" 'Dude, that was a fantastic shot to eighteen."

Skip took time off from his PGA apprenticeship in 1947 to play on the tour. He almost had to since there was money on the ground, and his scores were so incredibly good everywhere and whenever he played. They stayed good; Alexander won the National Capital and the Tucson Open in 1948, earning $2,000 for each; not a fortune, but rather good money when a new Buick Special cost $1,950 and gas was 22 cents a gallon. Skip said that the post-World War II vehicle tour "was just a bunch of vagabonds." "A tight-knit group that cuts the same pie every week." To generate a profit, you had to finish in the top ten every week. Skip did it. When Alexander was named to the Ryder Cup team in 1949, he had to cross the Atlantic on the Queen Elizabeth and wear the same blazer and pants as Sam Snead, Jimmy Demaret, and Ben Hogan, the non-playing captain, who was still weak and shaky from his car accident. Skip competed in one match, the foursomes, and fell to the Yanks 7-5 at Ganton Golf Club in Yorkshire, England. Making the US golf All-Star team, however, did not diminish his achievement.

The following year's car/hotel/golf course marathon was a little different because Skip and Kitty, aka Kathleen, had given birth to a baby girl Bunkie, aka Carol Ann. What the devil, they bought a suitcase that doubled as a crib for the infant, and the three Alexanders hit the road. Skip murdered 'em again, despite the additional stimulus. He won another tournament and a lot of money in 1950, and he appeared like a lock to compete in the next Ryder Cup. That was fantastic because the '51 Match was going to be contested at Pinehurst #2, which was probably his favourite course. As previously stated, he had won the North and South.

After finishing sixth at the Kansas City Open in September 1950, Alexander desperately wanted to return to North Carolina for a little visit before embarking on an exhibition tour of South America. He couldn't get a flight, but a Civil Air Patrol member offered to take him part of the way home; he had a tiny plane flying to Louisville. Skip was a rising star on the tour, and as a US Army Air Corps veteran (the CAP is the United States Air Force's civilian auxiliary), he had status. Sure, the huge man replied, I'd like a ride to Louisville. Thank you, Dude.

"Mayday, mayday, mayday." Something went wrong with the gas tank on the Beechcraft T-7 around eight p.m., at six thousand feet, about 130 miles from Louisville. The pilot shifted to the auxiliary tank, but it also didn't work. The four guys on board braced themselves; they'd try to fly the ten miles to Evansville, Indiana's airstrip. The silver-painted twin-engine prop plane hovered low over the tents of striking International Harvester employees before crashing dangerously near to the runway. Skip kicked a door open, got out of the plane, hopped a few painful feet, then collapsed, despite having a shattered ankle and a fractured leg, and being on fire. Ralph Reutter, a hero, rolled him around to smother the flames and removed his still-burning shoe and sock. The T-7's backup tank detonated moments later, killing the other three crew.

"He spent the next seven months in hospitals," says Buddy Alexander, son of the 1986 US Amateur champion and coach of the Florida Gators men's golf teams that won NCAA championships in

1993 and 2001. "They took so much skin from his rear end for grafts that his ass looked like a pair of madras pants."

Half of his ears had been charred by a gasoline fire. His torn and scarred skin had the gritty appearance of poured candle wax. But it was his hands... out of the seventy percent of his body that had been scorched, the man's hands were the worst. They'd darkened and curled almost into fists as they burnt. Early on, the doctors recommended amputation, at least of the pinky fingers. "My hands were all burned, and now they're all skin-grafted," Skip recalled. My fingers were so tight that I didn't have any gaps."

The patient's desire to play golf again seemed irrational, but he had an idea. Perhaps the surgeons could open his hands into a golf grip by cutting some tendons and removing some knuckles. It was worthwhile to give it a shot. Wilson, Alexander's equipment business, created a small five iron with a standard grip for the surgeons to use as a template in the OR. The club's head was emblazoned with the words "Little Dude."

At the next Masters, the scarred man was taken to a seat of honour: a chair in the shade of the long-leaf pines on the green, green grass between the twelfth green and the thirteenth tee, where no one is ever allowed except players and caddies. Old acquaintances greeted him cordially, and at least one of them must have noticed a tear in his eye.

Alexander was the penultimate qualifier for the 1951 Ryder Cup team, based wholly or nearly entirely on points gained prior to the plane disaster. It seems strange now, but back then—and it didn't change until 1963—the format called for 36-hole foursomes matches on day one and 36-hole singles matches on day two, then let's have a drink. Another twist to the 1951 tournament was an off day in the middle. The North Carolina Tar Heels football team hosted number one ranked Tennessee. That day, no one was going to watch golf.

Fans of the Tar Heels didn't witness much football either, as they were defeated 27-0 by the Vols.

That night, Captain Sam Snead called a meeting. Team USA was leading by three points to one, thus the outcome was still in doubt. It was time to discuss strategy.

"Skip was disappointed that he didn't get to play on the first day," Buddy explains. "He thought that if he played at all, it would be an alternate shot." It was for the best. Even if he only had to hit every other shot, his hands couldn't handle the abuse.

Captain Snead, on the other hand, had a problem: one of his stalwarts, Dutch Harrison, had phoned in ill. Skip, how about you? Sam stated. Do you want to play? No way, said Hogan, a guy who knew from experience. He can't go 36 miles. Snead's plan was simple: Alexander wouldn't have to play well or even finish. He'd be the scapegoat since he'd have to face the opposing team's finest player, John "Gentleman John" Panton, a popular Scot who had won practically everything except the Open. He'd have a drink named after him, like Arnold Palmer. A John Panton cocktail is made with ginger beer, bitters, and lime syrup.

The insanely motivated athlete tried it, but the thin, fragile skin on his hands didn't hold, and he bled profusely—through bandages, two sets of gloves, and onto his grips. Near the end, he ran out of towels to bleed into, and his legs ached. "Every time I played a hole, I wondered if I could play the next," he later explained.

Alexander's mere presence on the tee was a small miracle; his victory, eight and seven, was a significant one. The singles margin was the greatest in Cup history. USA 9 ½ GB 2 ½.

That early November day was his last hurrah. Alexander continued to compete in events over the next few years, but his career as a travelling pro ended. He spent the rest of his career as the golf pro at Lakewood Country Club in Florida, which was later renamed St. Petersburg Country Club.

"I guess it's a pretty similar story to Hogan, except Skip was hurt a little worse," his son says. "However, Dad didn't linger on his lost career. He always thought of himself as the luckiest man alive. Because he was still alive."

Skip was the one. Everyone adored Skip.

Tiger's return to the top may have been equally as difficult as his previous climb. Let's see what we think after another look at it.

CHAPTER 2

GOODBYE WORLD

Tiger made his new relationship public in front of everyone, following some white lies and misdirection. It wasn't the same as a movie star's former running into his new lover on a red carpet, but given the high profile of the people involved, as well as the money and egos, it was comparable.

"Hank, good luck," Claude "Butch" Harmon advised Henry "Hank" Haney. "It's a difficult squad to be a part of. And it's more difficult than it appears."

The historic meeting on the green carpet—the practice tee—at the 2004 Masters represented a significant shift in the life of the new teacher of record. First and foremost, Haney might say goodbye to home and hearth in suburban Dallas. For the following six years, he'd average 110 days per year of actual, physical contact with Woods, either at the boss's home in Florida or on the road at a tournament— never, as far as I know, at one of Hank's practice sites in north Texas. Another hundred or more nights would pass with a text message or a phone call. The discourse would be about Tiger's grip, Tiger's right elbow at impact, Tiger's toes at the head of the buffet line, after the briefest prelude about the NBA or whatever. When it was all said and done, Haney estimated they had roughly 1,200 chats about the same topic. Tiger was an incredibly reliant pupil.

The new guy would be paid $50,000 per year. Peanuts. When you consider the expense of nearly four months of flying fares, rental vehicles, Egg McMuffins, and hotel rooms, as well as the human cost of being away from home all that time, it's less than peanuts. Yes, Haney would receive a $25,000 bonus if Tiger won a major—he'd win six on Hank's watch—but just being connected with the finest player in the world was worth everything. Haney's reputation, credibility, and hourly rate would soar. He didn't believe he was underpaid. But it wasn't all one-putts and sand saves behind the scenes. The interaction between the choreographer and the prima ballerina was strong and complex from the outset. Haney eventually quit because he felt humiliated.

"It's a tough team to be on," Butch had previously stated.

The first rule of this team is to be modest. Author Tom Callahan disclosed the main cause of Butch's firing in his 2010 book, His Father's Son: it appears Earl and Tiger were watching golf on TV when coach Harmon came on and used a plural pronoun to describe several dramatic golf incidents. For example, "we hit a cut six iron in there pin high" and "we really needed to get off to a good start today."

Tiger then looked to Earl and asked, "We?"

Steinie, Stevie, Keith, Hank, and Tiger made up the new team. Steinie—IMG representative and BFF Mark Steinberg—fielded the offers and safeguarded his man like a hen with one chick. Among media types, he was known as Dr. No—as in, we will not comment on the rumours, and no, you cannot have two minutes with Tiger, and no, no, and no. Stevie—Steve Williams—had apparently not agreed with Butch; the gung-ho Kiwi defended the boss's body with energy on the golf course and fearlessly and competently performed the caddie duty. Keith Kleven, the owner and director of the D. Keith Kleven Institute of Orthopaedic (the British spelling) Sports and Dance Rehabilitation in Las Vegas, was an expert in constructing strong bodies in at least twelve ways. Earl and Elin, Tiger's fiancée, were two more you would have imagined were key characters in 2004 but weren't. Earl had hung on as long as he could in his son's professional life, but Tiger now had the immense strength of IMG and the tip of the spear in Steinberg. So, despite his generally poor health, Pops stayed at home and lived a sybarite's existence, paying the masseuse's expenses with money from his work as the Tiger Woods Foundation's president. Ms. Nordegren was and would remain in a lead-lined, walled-off section of her future husband's life.

"The toughest guy on the team was Tiger," Hank would later write. "One common misperception was that he was more knowledgeable about the golf swing than any modern player. Though Tiger had a lot of information, he'd proven that it wasn't enough to help him cure himself."

Hank would write: Thankfully, inquisitive minds like ours prompted Haney to compose a memoir of his six years on the squad. The fact that his career began with fame and concluded with tragedy lends structure and momentum to his narrative, but The Big Miss wouldn't be the amusing book it is without Haney's ghost, Golf Digest Senior Writer Jaime Diaz. Diaz was in a bind when he was offered the job, so he didn't take it straight immediately. Despite the fact that there was considerable money up front and the opportunity for more based on sales—the publisher's aspirations of a steady stream of revenue were realised when the book reached number one on the New York Times bestseller list—there were other factors to consider. "It ended my relationship with Tiger," Diaz said the instant he accepted the arrangement. Permanently."

Even the smallest amount of connection with the biggest man in golf, if not all sports, was gold for writers and broadcasters. This frequently resulted in a kid glove, let's-not-offend-Tiger press that was an affront to the First Amendment. Most reporters were afraid to ask probing questions. Jimmy Roberts and John Feinstein were notable outliers. Diaz, too. His strong interpersonal skills prevented the frequently bored and overly careful interviewee from clamming up or repeating another cliché. Diaz understood what he was talking about; he'd known the Woods family for years, and Tiger's mother liked him. That was beneficial.

"When Tiger's fame caused him to limit his time with writers, I took no offence," Diaz adds. "[However], for nine years, I interviewed him once a year for what we [at Golf Digest] termed 'The State of Tiger.' It was derisively referred to as a "house job," but I thought it was quite good."

It was. The fifth annual instalment, which coincided with Tiger's thirtieth birthday, for example, disclosed at least one "I didn't know that " aspect of the world's greatest golfer's worldview. "It's hard to make the ball move," Woods added, referring to how tough it had become to purposefully twist the orb in a meaningful way. He yearned for the days when "innovations" in equipment dumbed down the game. "You look at the old guys who were or are true shot-makers, like when I played at Bighorn with Lee Trevino and he blew my mind with some of the shots he hit." Then you look at the tour and wonder, "Who are the true shot-makers?" Who moves the ball or does something new with it?' And there aren't many, if any, out here any longer.``

If Tiger were to dominate the golf world, he would reintroduce spin to the ball, "so misses would be more pronounced and good shots would be more rewarded." He'd also ban wedges with more than 56 degrees of loft to add diversity to the short game. "Nobody hits half shots anymore," he explained. Diaz described it as a "house job," owing to Tiger's long association with Golf Digest. Their long and mainly positive relationship began in 1990. The founder of the host club addressed a sensitive subject about membership in an interview with the Birmingham Post-Herald before the 1990 PGA Championship. "I think we've said that we don't discriminate in every area except blacks," Hall Thompson remarked, and thus the Shoal Creek Controversy was created. From that point forward, host courses for tour events and majors had to be open about their membership policies.

"After Shoal Creek, we published a two-part series on discrimination at private clubs," says Jerry Tarde, Editor-in-Chief of Golf Digest.

"We tried to play a positive role in welcoming minorities to golf." We collaborated with John Merchant [a black USGA official] and hosted several symposia with black golf leaders. Earl Woods was one of them.

"Earl and I played golf together and got to know each other. Fast forward through his son's six national titles, and there's a wild rush to sign him when he gets pro. That's exactly what we do. The best, like Jack Nicklaus and Seve [Ballesteros], write for us. But George Peper [then-editor of Golf Magazine, Digest's competitor] recognized an opportunity to snag the best guy. Not only is he the best guy, but he is also the new face of golf. There was a heated recruitment process.

"During the 1996 Masters, I had many conversations with Earl. We went to a jazz club in downtown Augusta one night. 'I truly need your assistance,' I explained. 'Don't worry, I'll handle everything,' he added."

And he did it. Tarde was pleased to note that Tiger's face on the cover boosted newsstand sales like no one else had or would, but as time passed, Woods found less and less time to be photographed hitting shots for the instructional pieces written by GD staffers Pete McDaniel, Guy Yocom, and Mark Soltau. This was a problem because the magazine's backbone was "how I hit the stinger'"—or the flop shot, or left-handed, or whatever.

According to Tarde, the thirteen-year partnership ended in 2010 due to a mutual decision made without animosity. But Team Tiger's relationship with Golf Digest Senior Writer Diaz was far from done. The parties had an unspoken agreement that Jaime would ghostwrite Tiger's autobiography (which Tiger wanted to write as much as he wanted to eat sand, which was not at all) and another instructive book. Would those prospects vanish if Diaz wrote a memoir for Hank the Disgruntled Instructor, or if he allowed it to be too honest? IMG, did you consider that idea before or during the drafting of the Haney book? Diaz would not reveal, but the other books did not take place. For Diaz had assisted Hank in breaching instructor/student privilege—which hadn't been a thing until now, because who cared about the back-and-forth between any other pair?

The Big Miss, which came out in 2012, two years after the Revelations, captivated me, and I recommend it, but if I hear another mention of "swing plane," I'm going to punch someone. The term "swing plane" was most likely invented by Anthony Ravielli, the portrait painter turned illustrator who created the graphics for Hogan's Five Lessons, the golf instructor's Bible. According to a conversation I had with the writer, the late Herbert Warren Wind, it was often an image first, then concept. Ravielli drew a pane of glass with Hogan in the centre, and teachers have been arguing about the "swing plane" ever since. Hank and Tiger saw value in the notion that appealing geometry was the key to the golf swing, whereas the majority of us, Hank, could benefit from instructive pieces titled "How to Win With Your Crappy Swing" and "Effective Choking." The perfection he and Tiger sought is irrelevant to the vast majority of the rest of us, an under-examined topic in the field of golf instruction. Diaz describes Haney as a fantastic colleague. The job of the ghost is tremendous when the putative author is uncommitted, inarticulate, or sluggish, but Hank came to the writing table with a comprehensive strategy and a feeling of mission. His motivation stemmed from the notion that he had been used as a scapegoat during difficult times and had received little recognition for his contribution to the team's success. The Big Miss was marketed as a "tell-all" book, but was it really more of a "tell-some?" What did you leave out, Mr. Diaz?

"The publisher was always pushing for more personal stuff, such as anything about Elin," Diaz explained. "Some readers were upset that the novel wasn't more explicit. On the other hand, golf professionals complained that it was too intimate. We determined that anything pertaining to Tiger's golf was fair game. And I believe we demonstrated that his peace of mind and self-esteem were severely harmed as a result of what he did."

21

Reviewers generally centred on the "popsicle incident," concluding that it demonstrated Tiger's shocking lack of interest in other people in frozen form, or that it demonstrated the tunnel vision of this specific great athlete. You may recall that after long days on the practice tee at Isleworth—which was within easy golf cart distance of Tiger's front door in his gated community in suburban Orlando—teacher and student would frequently retire to Casa de Tiger. Tiger would head to his Sub Zero after supper, with the game on the huge screen, and withdraw a solitary sugar-free popsicle; I've always imagined an orange one. And that was the end of Tiger's actions. He'd suck and taste his'sicle while Hank stood there watching. The naïve host never provided a frozen dessert to his guest, who desired one but felt awkward asking for it.

According to The Big Miss, when Steinie told Hank that Tiger considered him one of his best pals, the instructor was taken aback. He considered but did not say: "I am?"

The popsicle and other examples of Tiger's slowed development exposed in The Big Miss, such as his taught inability to pick up a dinner tab or just say thank you, and moody silences as sullen as a teenager's gloom, should be contrasted with some of the champion's extremely positive attributes. He was a modest individual who was a fair competitor and athlete. He took his generosity very seriously (and generously endowed his charities). Only a few of his other tour players knew him—Tiger didn't blend in—but they liked him and respected his brave reaction to pressure. And they liked how popular he'd made the sport, which made them all a shitload of money. When he first joined the tour, purses were at $101 million; twelve years later, in 2008, the figure was $292 million. But Tiger's desire to put in the work must rank first in his plus column. He worked hard for his accomplishment. He put in a lot of effort.

Not to go all Gary Smith on you, but consider yourself in Tiger's shoes for a moment. Assume it's mid-April 2005. Smith's psychiatrist's couch technique was on full display in his long, melodramatic profile of heavyweight champ and heavyweight psychopath Mike Tyson for Sports Illustrated—in the second person. "You take your pigeons out of their cages one at a time and release them." "You wish you could fly, too"—something along those lines. That's something I can't do.

Tiger was chosen Sportsman of the Year in 1996, and The Sports Whisperer used his affecting but slightly creepy approach to write the magazine's Sportsman of the Year essay (he'd be named SI's S.O.Y. again in 2000). But back then, Earl approached the microphone or the shadow of a writer's attention like a drunk seeking for a drink, and he was overjoyed with claims that his son—no ordinary golfer, that boy—would unify the countries. Earl, really— nations? Yes, he said it again, the nations. Tiger had little to say; he was a shadow of the man he'd become a decade later.

In this imagined moment, Tiger is sitting on his couch. He stops, thoughtfully, between watching a DVD of a documentary he's seen so many times he knows it by heart and a shooting game he's played hundreds of times. He thinks back a few days to the previous Sunday afternoon, when he was leading the Masters by one shot with three holes to go, but his engine was leaking so much 10W-30 that it almost seized. On sixteen, the snow globe short hole with a reflecting pond between the tee and the green, he'd hit a terrible pull hook. He'd given Stevie a glance.

"Can you tell me where that is?"

"There's a long way to go."

"What's going on over there?"

"I'm not sure. I've never been there before. I've never looked there before."

Tiger's ball has come to rest in an unfavourable location. Lush rough behind his Nike TW One Platinum complicated the shot significantly, but the Masters won't let you call it rough: it's the "first cut." Also, people are patrons, not individuals.

Tiger psychologically immerses himself in the moment's struggle while announcers Verne Lundquist and Lanny Wadkins whisper their analyses. He uses self-belief and discipline to his advantage. He removes the fear inhibition. He lifts his ball to an exact square inch of firm ground, and the ball glides very slowly sideways down the hill toward the hole through the sun-dappled shade or the shade-dappled sun, the patrons' sound increasing with each inch. The ball pauses, as if fatigued from its descent, before falling over the lip and into the hole. As Tiger and Stevie dance around and punch the air, the audience roars and Verne Lundquist loses it ("Oh, wow!" Verne exclaims, not exactly a call for the ages). They make an effort at a high five but fail.

Even positive thinking and controlled breathing won't help much if your swing seems like it belongs on someone else's body, like secondhand clothing. Tiger shot his drive so far right on seventeen after his amazing chip that his ball almost reached the fairway on fifteen. Bogey. On hole eighteen, he sent his three-wood tee shot into the left rough—his fourth miss of the fairway in the final five holes. The Nike TW One Platinum splashed into brilliant white bunker sand after he went well right with his iron shot. "God. "Dammit!" shouted the competitor, and the CBS-TV audio was perfectly clear. Another bogey, and I'm tied with the tenacious, unlucky (he lipped out his chip on 18) Chris DiMarco.

But Tiger won the playoff with three immaculate strokes for eagle on the first playoff hole—eighteen again. He'd now won the Masters four times. The aftermath had been out of the ordinary. For one thing, he had a wife to hug—he and the stunning former nanny had married six months ago, in a quiet, private wedding in Barbados that had cost millions. I'm not sure what the helicopter rental rates were, but the Woods Forward Nuptials Team leased every known Barbadian chopper to thwart the paparazzi air force. The Team also paid one and a half million dollars to rent the entire resort where the wedding took place. Now here was the lovely blonde Elin in hugging posture, dressed in designer shades and a red top to match his own Sunday fighting attire.

Earl was not present for his traditional, lengthy embrace. That was unique. Instead of attending the training, he sat in his hotel room watching TV. The aftermath of the incident was routine. Steinie did his hardest, but he couldn't block out all the noise, grabbing hands, and waiting expressions. And the media was a real headache. Celebrity, Tiger discovers, is corrosive, like a constant trickle of acid on his life. His privacy has disappeared like fog in the sun. Everywhere he goes, all eyes are on him, giving the impression that he is being trivialised, as if he is a roadside attraction. Look, Tiger! Kathy, please come to a halt! Arnold Palmer is the only other golfer in history who made people swoon when he entered a room, but Arnie always liked it. He'd shake the man's hand, sign the autograph, smile, and mean it. But Tiger's personality and circumstances are vastly different from Arnie's. He has to forge his own path. But, while his life has altered, he has not. What makes him tick— something he's expressed many times and that people still don't completely understand—is his quest to discover what's possible. Is it possible to be the best ever? It was doable for Bobby Jones, Ben Hogan, and Jack Nicklaus. As a result, they can be exceeded. Tiger is now pondering the benefits of being a global star. Let's see: there's the plane, the yacht, this house, this couch, and the dive boat. The V-VIP service in Vegas is quite nice. Elin? Marriage is... OK. Hank thinks her smile is getting smaller and smaller every time he sees her. Maybe. Maybe a lot of things. He may live other lives. It is possible. Tiger takes up the remote. Play is pressed.

"There are no timeouts in war, no staged popularity contests to decide life and death," a solemn voice says over scenes of beaches, explosions, and green-painted troops in camo firing automatic guns. "This program is about the eighty-three young men of Class 234 and their six-month struggle to become US Navy SEALS in a training course called Basic Underwater Demolition SEAL Training, or BUD/S."

Navy SEALs: BUD/S Class 234 is a six-part, four-hour and twenty-minute documentary from 2002 that depicts a rigorous weeding out procedure. On a beach, a shivering, tired sailor must hold a downward-facing dog stance as an instructor shovels sand on his ass. Teams of seven manoeuvre rubber boats into 54-degree ocean water and surfable waves. again after again, the maybe-SEALs are defeated. Then they do it at night. They run four miles on the beach, mostly failing to meet the required time of thirty-two minutes or less. They hold heavy poles overhead until their arms shake, then do it again. Some people inhale water and almost drown during underwater swimming sessions.

During "motivational timeouts," candidates perform hundreds of pushups as an instructor sprays them on the head with a hose and yells. "You don't give in to pain; you adapt to it!"

Another common interchange is:

Teacher: Do you know what second place is?

Potential SEAL: First loser!

"The main lesson of Phase One: individuals cannot survive in wartime," says the solemn voice-over. "No matter how high the surf or how wet and cold they become, Class 234 must develop trust in teamwork." Trust in one another is a necessary SEAL attribute for survival."

That would be nice, Tiger thinks, to be part of a stealthy, violent, and anonymous squad rather than a lonely single performance, which he is, despite the in-air-quotes "team" of Steinie and Hank and the others. Could he forgo fame, golf, a $60 million mortgage, a $50 million (on its way to $100 million) annual endorsement money, and the constraints of golf and matrimony? Is that possible? Tiger now envisions the covert life in a different light. He sets down the remote, puts on his headphones, and takes up the PlayStation controller. SOCOM: US Navy SEALs are ready to go. It's "a tactical shooter game emphasising stealth and slow pacing to complete the objective and neutralise the enemy." According to Wikipedia, "it is intended to simulate realistic combat." According to my son John, an expert in this field, SOCOM: US Navy SEALs is really decent and a little bit harder than the typical game. Yes, Tiger thinks, but he's not thinking clearly. What I believe he believes is that the rewards for his sacrifice and achievement are insufficient. Perhaps severe self-indulgence can alleviate the emptiness. He has the perfect cover to fool his wife and everyone else. He needs to go out of town on business a lot, and he has his own jet, a Plutonium credit card, fame, terrific teeth, and, as it would turn out, a slew of girls who wanted to tag along. He takes up his phone. He's getting a text. Jaimee.

Tiger's fantasy existence was shattered when his father died on May 3, 2006. Earl Woods, 74, died at his home in Cypress, California, a suburb of Los Angeles. With his diabetes, poor circulation, and cardiac problems, he was 74 years old. In 2004, his prostate cancer returned. Earl Dennison Woods was born on March 5, 1932, in Manhattan, Kansas, as the sixth of six children. His father worked as a mason. He was orphaned at the age of thirteen, and he was survived by his wife Kultida, three children from a previous marriage, Earl, Jr. of Phoenix, Kevin of Los Angeles, and Royce Woods of San Jose, California. Following the prodigy's death, a wealth of information about his father became available. Little of it is flattering, particularly his philandering, which Tiger was well aware of and despised. Tarde of Golf Digest offers an informative and humorous summary:

"Regarding Earl: I'm reminded of Bogart and the young girl Annina's wonderful exchange in Casablanca." 'Monsieur Rick, what kind of man is Captain Renault?' she asks. 'Oh, he's just like any other man,' Bogart responds. "Only more so."We're all flawed, and maybe I'm being too gentle with Earl. I knew him as a friend—he was dependable, loving, hilarious, and incredibly intelligent. We all have a special admiration for those who have served their country in the military. He served two tours of duty in Vietnam, the second with the United States Army Special Forces. "I thought there was a part of Tiger that was always trying to measure up."

"We were a religious sect consisting of two people," James Marcus wrote in the New Yorker, describing the void in his own life after his father's death. Half of the congregation had already left." That also applied to Tiger to some extent. At the very least, he'd lost his best friend.

Tiger's poise as he eulogised his father at the Tiger Woods Learning Center in Anaheim, which had opened three months previously, astonished Haney. Then what? What now? Tiger's reaction to his father's death remains unknown. Events overlap and intersperse in our lives, much like melting Neapolitan ice cream. We could divide Tiger's trip in the years leading up to and following Earl's death into three sections: golf, SEALs, and that other thing. But these three activities did not occur in order; they merged to form his single life. It's astonishing that he managed to keep all three of these big balls in the air. Tiger clearly mourned, felt hurt, and was disrupted, despite his poker face, but look at how he played! Earl's son won the Open Championship at Royal Liverpool a few months after Earl died, and then every tournament he participated in for the remainder of the year. Another major one during this six-win stretch was the PGA Championship at Medinah. It was his twelfth major championship.

Tiger's emotions erupted on the eighteenth green at Royal Liv. "[He] fell into my arms and wouldn't let go," Caddie Williams said in his book Out of the Rough. "I instinctively moved away from him—his victory hugs were traditionally short and sweet—but as I tried to break free, his embrace tightened and I realised this wasn't the Tiger I knew." He couldn't stop sobbing. I'd never seen him look like this before."

Stevie would have to fill in for Earl in the hugging area at the very least. In 2006, Tiger won eight times. In 2007, he won seven more tournaments, including the PGA Championship at Southern Hills for the second time. In 2007, his adjusted (for golf course difficulty) stroke average was 67.79 (more italics, please). That tied Tiger's 2000 total for the lowest ever (Nelson averaged 68 points in his big year, 1945; adjusted average is a new thing). However, statistics cloud the picture. Superlatives pile up and lose their meaning. I like to imagine Tiger as a young man wearing a Hootie and the Blowfish t-shirt with a backward-facing ballcap. He's flashing his tombstone teeth and mocking his elders, who are sitting in rocking recliners and dressed in lap blankets, flannel, dandruff, and heavy spectacles. It seems a shame to simply recap Tiger's outstanding game throughout these glory years, particularly his legendary 91-hole victory at Torrey Pines in the 2008 US Open. The angels sang that week for Rocco Anthony Mediate, a cheerful chap from wild Western Pennsylvania who played the game with a weak back and an unappealing but functional golf swing and had won five times on the tour. In other words, when Rocco Anthony Mediate was on, he could really play. Tiger matching him after four rounds was extraordinary because he was only using one anterior cruciate ligament, half the typical allotment, and he also had a couple of hairline cracks in his tibia. A post-Master's operation for "cleaning up" the bothersome left knee had discovered the major structural issues. Woods walked as if he had spear grass in his socks that week, and the act of following through was painful. Tiger's "Hogan at Merion" moment had arrived. He swung at a ball midway through the second round, right before Destiny made Tiger it's kid and put the hole in the path of a chip or two and lots and lots of long, long putts, and it wounded him so much that he appeared to be in tears.

"Is it really worth it, Tiger?" said Stevie.

"Fuck you, I'm winning this tournament," the one-legged golfer answered.

Rocco impersonated Tiger in the eighteen-hole playoff by wearing a red shirt and black pants. Tiger was not joking when he quipped, "Nice fucking shirt," during the warm-up. "Last clean one I had," Rocco responded. Or did it?

In the case, neither Woods nor the moment daunted Mediate; they played another eighteen holes and tied again. Tiger parred the sudden death hole and then went to visit his surgeon. His knee and leg problems have gotten worse. Tiger underwent his first operation on the union of the thigh bone and the shinbone as a freshman for excision of scar tissue and a benign (non-cancerous) cyst, the cyst being a little bag of joint fluid that formed on the back of his knee. It occurred as a result of prolonged leaking caused by chronic inflammation caused by repeated strong swings at golf balls. The darn thing reappeared, as it often does, and Tiger needed another cystectomy in 2002. With that one enormous joint in mind, he decided to adjust his swing once again. It has to be less stressful in some way. Hank Haney's original charge when they met in 2004 was to find Tiger a new, knee-friendly stroke. Perhaps his training was to blame; perhaps it had gained a new edge and intensity. Tiger had been exceeding the weight of the weights his trainer, Keith Kleven, preferred by orders of magnitude in his praiseworthy enthusiasm to get stronger and win more golf tournaments—or from a preening self-regard and desire to seem good for the other gender. Kleven advocated for a large number of reps. Tiger believed that moving large weights fast was ideal for him. Perhaps it was his swing, not just the frequency with which he used it, that caused the injury. Tiger's style included a manoeuvre known as "posting up," which involves straightening the left leg at or immediately after impact. Posting up enhances the distance the ball will fly in the correct hands, but a straight leg doesn't absorb shock effectively, according to my ski instructor, so a mogul bump or the tension of weight transfer in a golf swing radiates into the knee ligaments, the spine, and the neck. Tiger became a (lowercase) wounded warrior as a result. Except for one year, he suffered mild to crippling injuries and seven surgeries every year from 2007 to 2019.

SEAL training could also have played a part in his physical breakdown. Tiger trained on an honorary basis, but it was real training, and therefore dangerous. He got badly bruised on the thigh by a rubber bullet and once got kicked hard in his already sore knee. Along with real Sea, Air, Land virtuosos of the killing arts, he jumped from planes, practised his hand-to-hand combat skills, simulated urban combat, and fired various weapons at various targets. Unsurprisingly, he proved to be a good shot. On his own, he ran and ran in combat boots, a weighted vest, and camo. He was already an expert diver; he was super-fit. His mental strength was through the roof. Tiger had all the attributes of a successful candidate, except one.

In 2007, when he was thirty-one, the erstwhile golfer trained on six occasions with the SEALs. Caddie Williams had known about his obsession for years; after a poor showing in the 2004 US Open, Tiger had pulled their car to the side of the road. "Stevie, I think I've had enough of golf," he said. "I'd really like to try to be a Navy SEAL." A SEAL? Steinie was incredulous. Haney was dubious. "Aren't you too old?" the teacher asked Tiger one day. Good question, because according to navy.com, "Navy SEAL recruits must be between the ages of seventeen to twenty-eight. There are some waivers for men ages twenty-nine and thirty that are available for very qualified candidates. These applicants must prove to the Navy and Navy SEAL community that they are worth the investment."

"It's not a problem," Tiger replied. "They're making a special age exception for me."

We wondered what a guy who'd been there and done that thought. Would Tiger have been able to make it through the training? Would he have been someone you'd want to fight beside?

"Yes," says Aaron Silton, a former Marine Corps Raider. Raiders are the rough equivalent of SEALs, Rangers, and Green Berets; an elite and especially lethal military force. "Tiger can do whatever he wants to do. Being a special operator is no more than a mindset. In training or on a mission, it's not being able to quit. And Tiger has no quit in him."

Woods wanted to transition from golfer to warrior; Silton did the opposite. His unlikely path to the first tee started in a firefight in a dusty little village in southwest Afghanistan in September 2009. He'd dispatched a dozen enemies, probably more, when a bullet fired by a Taliban sniper from a Dragunov rifle found Silton's head. The finger-sized shell tunnelled through his cheek, teeth, tongue, and neck before lodging in the butt stock of his machine gun. Fellow Marines pulled Silton out of the hot orange sand and the bee-infested thorn bush he'd had fallen into, but too roughly—severely dislocating his shoulder. It got worse: on the operating table in Kandahar, Silton suffered a massive stroke. And a harried medic needlessly stuck surgical staples into his scrotum. Damn. What was the worst part of his life after that? The surgeries, the months in bed with a jaw wired shut, the slurred speech, the anger, the obsession with returning to Afghanistan to blow away the motherfucker who'd shot him? Or was it the PTSD? After months in Walter Reed National Military Medical Center—where he became friends with comedian Jon Stewart, a good-hearted man for visiting wounded vets—Aaron was transferred to Camp Pendleton in San Diego for more months of rehab. He and his wife lived off base. It didn't go well. Silton wouldn't, couldn't leave home without his Remington Tango 1-MT knife on his hip.

"Dinners were OK," Silton says. "Parties, no. I had a short fuse. I could get into physical violence very quickly."

Recalls Tiffany, his wife: "We had to stop going anywhere."

That could have been Tiger's life if he had chosen to forego fortune and celebrity in order to serve his country by participating in its conflicts. There was a recent case of a professional athlete doing just that. Pat Tillman, the Arizona Cardinals' hard-hitting strong safety, was so upset by the 9/11 tragedy that he resolved to do something about it. He performed admirably during his fourth football season in 2001, so well that the organisation offered him a three-year contract worth a million point two per year, more than doubling his salary. Instead, Tillman followed through on his vow, enrolled in June 2002, and became another kind of badass, an Army Ranger, before being deployed to Iraq and Afghanistan. In April 2004, he was murdered by friendly fire. Where Men Win Glory, Jon Krakauer's book about Tillman's journey, is a must-read. The irony to Silton's story: One day in recovery, he was given a pair of golf clubs—he'd never hit a ball before, except for some home run swings with his high school mates at a driving range back home in suburban Boston. "This game sucks," the Raider stated. "Why would anyone want to play it?" But the rush he felt with each clean hit on his second shot at golf drove his incredible comeback. The man with the bullet in his head is now a golf instructor in Carlsbad with a whole instruction book. He's also a fantastic golfer with a zero handicap and competitive goals. It's yet another incredible golf comeback.

Tiger Woods, Silton's golf star, played bravely after yet another round of surgery on his questionable knee, but then began his long fall from Mount Olympus. Woods led the 2009 PGA Championship at Hazeltine with one round to play, which meant he was a lock to win the 2009 PGA Championship at Hazeltine. In his career, he had fifty 54-hole leads or ties for the lead and had won 47 of those competitions. On Sunday, the runner-up will most certainly be a round-faced man from Seoul with the Americanized moniker Y. E. Yang.

Yang Yong-eun, 37, the son of a farmer of the volcanic soil of Jeju-do—South Korea's Hawaii, its Honeymoon Island—had discovered golf late in life. His world rating had been 460 at the start of the year, but he'd won the Honda Classic in the spring—"from out of nowhere," as they say—and his number was now practically in the double digits. By that moment, the world's number one golfer had won seventy professional tournaments. Yang had only won one.

On that Saturday night, someone asked the world's 110th-ranked player what he believed his chances of winning were.

"About seventy to one," he calculated.

Several reports of the day claim that Tiger and Stevie tried to annoy YY by never saying anything to him, violating his space by standing too near, and playing very slowly when the pressure was on. If they did all of that, it was out of character and failed. Y-Squared seized a one-shot lead when he chipped in for eagle on fourteen, a short par four. On hole fifteen, he told his caddie, "Tiger is nervous." Someone afterwards inquired as to why the South Korean man was not nervous. "It's not like you're fighting Tiger in an octagon and he's going to bite you or swing at you with his nine iron." "The worst thing I could do was lose to Tiger," Yang Yong-eun jokes. Then he told the untruth that every underdog tells.

"So I didn't have much at stake."

There is nothing to lose and nothing to gain! Hilarious!

With a thrilling birdie on the final hole—remember that hybrid from 210 over the tree and over a bunker to a tight pin on eighteen?—the hitherto unknown Y. E. Yang defeated Tiger Damn Woods for the day and won the PGA by three shots. It was even closer; Tiger bogeyed the final two holes in desperate bids to make birdie. Nonetheless, Tiger's round of 75 was two strokes higher than any of his fourteen major victories. Over the fourteen final rounds, he averaged 69.5. The other guy thumping his fist on the eighteenth green seemed strange, impossible. Three months later, a considerably more serious setback occurred.

Tiger, as you know, had this wild third life that ate up the other two. I find myself uninterested in recalling the twists and turns of the Revelations of Sexual Misconduct. Furthermore, other sources, such as current issues of the National Enquirer, provide a considerably more complete and impassioned retelling than I could ever provide. But was there anything credible about this newspaper cartoon? I know I want to read headlines like "Mel Gibson: My Life as a Rabbit," "Al Gore's Diet is Making Him Stupid," and "Dying Man's Last Words Are Winning Lottery Numbers," but I won't accept the bunny story until Mel tells me about it.

Regardless of the validity of its reporting, the National Enquirer had actual power and influence, as well as a sizable budget to fund its small army of spies (as you surely know, paying sources is strictly prohibited in genuine journalism). For example, the Enquirer's mercenary tattletales snuffed out the presidential aspirations of Democratic up-and-comers Gary Hart and John Edwards—an affair and an out-of-wedlock child—and tarnished Rev. Jesse Jackson's reputation by confirming the existence of his "love child." The grist for its mill is sex, murder (thank you, OJ), the British royal family, and various celebrity calamities. The tsk-tsk sex stories in the tabloid have an almost Puritanical tinge.

Who are the people who read it? In almost all those words, the parent company's CEO remarked in 2017: "Our readers are losers." "These are people who live their lives failing, so they want to read negative things about people who have gone up and then come down," David Pecker stated in an interview with the New Yorker, seemingly certain that his casual insult would not be picked up on by his readers. As you may recall, Pecker was a significant figure in the Donald Trump/Stormy Daniels saga.

Tiger had been on the cover of the National Enquirer since 2007. It was their standard procedure: a tipter dropped a dime (in this case, the girl's mother); their operatives surveilled; and then, bingo, the subject was seen canoodling in his Escalade with someone who wasn't called Elin. A "catch and kill" deal was supposedly struck. Tiger consented to a cover story for the Enquirer's sister journal, Men's Fitness, in which he revealed the mechanics of his previously unknown training routine in exchange for the Enquirer's pledge not to publish "sin-sational!" phrases and photographs.

Something similar happened to the aforementioned Rachel two years later. "She's dating Tiger," someone at the supermarket tabloid muttered, and soon sharp-eyed individuals were following her, even to Melbourne, where the Australian Masters was being played and Tiger was competing. To write a thorough biography, Keteyian and Benedict had to lay it all out in Tiger Woods. I didn't, but squeamish readers might like Chapters 28 and 29. "People who like this sort of thing will find this the sort of thing they like," Abraham Lincoln said, maybe referring to something written by Walt Whitman, perhaps Leaves of Grass: "People who like this sort of thing will find this the sort of thing they like."

You've heard the basic story. Elin examined her sleeping husband's cell phone for evidence on Thanksgiving night, sparked by the Rachel/Australia story in the Enquirer. She became so enraged that she roused her mate, resulting in a fight. It was two o'clock in the morning. Tiger's mother came to see... He crashed his black SUV while fleeing Elin. Mrs. Woods smashed both of the car's rear windows with a nine iron for reasons that are still unknown. Were there enough clubs?

I returned to the crash scene much later. On that crisp, bright winter morning, teams of uniformed landscapers clipped and primped the lovely lawns of Isleworth, while the drone of leaf blowers filled the air. I was struck by how magnificent and spacious the residences were, as well as how quickly the big Caddy had to be travelling to sideswipe a fire hydrant and T-bone a tree, a robust live oak. Everyone has moved on after a decade, but back then—well. The consequences were catastrophic.

Within two weeks, thirteen additional mistresses emerged, at least one of whom had been bribed to keep their big mouths shut. It was an ideal storm for the Enquirer—and, to be sure, for the non-celebrity-scandal media—because it was a slow-rolling tragedy, like a serial, with new ex-lovers from the food and beverage sector and party ladies and "actresses" surfacing as Tiger inamorata day after day.

Tiger was discarded by sponsors as if he were radioactive, hot, and stinky. Accenture, a technology consultancy firm located in Ireland, stated slán. AT&T bid Tiger farewell. Gatorade and Gillette both ended their contracts. The association with Golf Digest also ended, but it has been tapering down since before the Revelations. Procter & Gamble and Swiss watchmaker Tag Heuer distanced themselves from its endorsement while not terminating their connection. Only two of his major contracts remained in place: those with Nike and EA Sports, the firm behind the enormously famous Tiger Woods PGA Tour video game.

The universe decided that Tiger had not had enough to deal with two weeks into the inferno. An examination into the practice of Tony Galea, a Canadian sports medicine expert who had made a visit to the Woods home in Orlando, became public. An alphabet soup of agencies—RCMP, FBI, ICE, DEA, and Homeland Security—were or would soon be investigating what Galea had in his needles and vials. That was human growth hormone, right? Steroids? Those are prohibited! Galea had a lot of success helping high-profile athletes recover from injuries, including Tiger Woods and his friend Alex Rodriguez, the legendary A-Rod.

Huge Humor roared to life as the Enquirer splashed huge, red numbers on its front page as shorthand for the mistress count—for example, 9!—on the main page. "Let's see what else is making headlines." Oh! Another mistress appeared today—how many are there now, Paul?"—and late-night monologists couldn't help but make a Tiger connection. Saturday Night Live mimicked CNN, with Jason Sudeikis as a stuttering Wolf Blitzer and Kenan Thompson as Tiger, who wore a golf club around his head and a tire track across his chest, apologising to faux-Elin (Blake Lively) for running himself over with the car. On another Saturday night, "Mistress #15" (Nasim Pedrad) is perplexed by a snapshot of the other Tiger paramours. "I just thought they were me in different outfits and hairs," she said, referring to how similar they looked: primarily blonde. Although some of the vixens may have been valedictorians, the humorous assumption was that they were all a little foolish.

Garry Trudeau created a series in his "Doonesbury" comic strip in which the Tiger women decide to join a union.

One of the most famous and successful athletes in history had devolved into a farce. There are worse things than being publicly ridiculed and laughed at, but they are few and far between.

It took a long time to tell the Tiger joke. It lasted because of pent-up envy, heaping on, a bit of racism, and a general just desserts attitude. Furthermore, as long as sex is involved, constant public brutality is acceptable in our magnificent country. Murderers have it easier. For example, how frequently did Jay Leno publicly embarrass Monica Lewinsky? Was there ever any acknowledgement by Jay and his authors that there was a human inside?

Tiger, on the other hand, was not amused. Elin moved away before Christmas to an unfurnished property nearby, taking the two kids with her. On Christmas Day, the four of them were together, and then Elin and the kids were off to Sweden, to her twin sister and soulmate, to her home and family. I imagine the unhappy pair felt soul-sick since they weren't together on New Year's Eve and worried if they'd ever be together again.

Tiger spent 45 days at a sex addiction facility in Hattiesburg, Mississippi, from late December to February 2010. Some assumed his Team was simply medicalizing the problem to give Tiger cover, but the sheer number of extra-marital partners and blatant disdain for his own and others' well-being argue otherwise. He was sick. Ari Fleischer, a former White House press secretary, was engaged by the Team to manage the problem. Steinie was adamantly opposed to the proposal, but Ari prevailed: apologise as totally and publicly as possible.

Tiger, clearly regretful, delivered a speech in a conference room at PGA Tour headquarters in Florida on February 19. It was one of those "stop the presses, turn on the TV" moments. The keynote speaker would have to talk about his sex life in front of his mother with cameras rolling, a punishment straight from hell.

"I am deeply sorry for my irresponsible and selfish behaviour," he apologised.

"I have failed you. "I have disappointed my fans.""I brought this on myself. "I've never used any performance-enhancing medications.

"It's not what you achieve in life that matters, but what you overcome."

His wedding? Everything is still up in the air. He was not going to say anything about it.

Tiger hugged his mother, Steinie, and close friend and Stanford golf teammate Notah Begay III after nearly fourteen minutes of solemn apologising. He then shook the hand of PGA Tour Commissioner Tim Finchem, who remained seated.

Stevie was watching from New Zealand, on the other side of the world. "Peculiar," he subsequently remarked. "He was so awkward in his delivery and word choice." Heavily contrived and lacking in naturalism... I'm sure it wasn't his idea. Those who knew him realised that it was not something he would do."

Some Tiger viewers were taken aback by his reference to religion near the end. "For me, Buddhism is part of following this path [of recovery]." "People probably don't realise that I was raised as a Buddhist and actively practised my faith from childhood until I drifted away from it in recent years."

People didn't realise it because Tiger had kept his religion a secret up until that point, but we believe this was the time to bring it up. Steps two, three, five, six, seven, and eleven of the surprisingly churchy (and Christian) Twelve Steps Program that many treatment programs embrace—including the one Tiger had just completed—concern the addict reaching out to God, recognizing that only God's help can see you through, that you are powerless without God, and so on.

However, as they seek enlightenment, Buddhists strive to adapt and improve as individuals. Buddhists do not believe in or worship a saviour. Only Six Steps would suffice for Patient Woods.

Other athletes have been involved in sex scandals. Baseball players Wade Boggs and Pete Rose, for example, suffered from sex addiction, but as great as those marvellously efficient singles hitters were, they were nowhere near defining their sport in the same way that Tiger did, and they were not in Tiger's league in ten other ways, including popularity, influence, and income. Has something like this ever happened before? Who else in American sports and entertainment history has sat as high as Tiger and been brought down by indiscretion, only to be pummelling by a happy, leering press?

While not exactly comparable, possibly O.J. Simpson (double murder)? Doping by Lance Armstrong? Mike Tyson (a rapist)? Michael Vick (cruelty to animals)? Ray Rice (domestic violence)? NBA great Kobe Bryant was publicly chastised for his infidelity (and nearly went to trial for rape), but his wife, Vanessa, supported him and he has since managed to rebuild his public image (and win an Oscar).

More lately, the "me too" movement has dragged down, justifiably, Hollywood icons such as Harvey Weinstein, Mario Batali, Kevin Spacey, and, perhaps most notoriously, Louis C.K. With the exception of O.J., who most certainly murdered two people, none of these cases drew the level of public interest that Tiger's did. To find a true comparison—at least in terms of media frenzy—you'd have to go back almost a century, when a man named Roscoe Arbuckle from Kansas suffered a similar fate.

Little Roscoe had a rough start in life because he was never truly small; despite the fact that both of his parents were tiny, slight folks, Baby Arbuckle came weighing a robust thirteen pounds. Because he loathed U.S. Senator Roscoe Conkling (R-NY), who had earned a national reputation as a womaniser, and because he believed the child was not his, the nominal father gave the child a nasty name: "Roscoe Conkling Arbuckle" chastised both the mother and the bouncing infant boy every minute of every day. When Mary Arbuckle died twelve years later, following the family's relocation to Santa Ana, California, William refused to support this enormous kid he disliked and had never claimed.

Whatever his genetic heritage, Roscoe possessed singing talent, the peculiar and amazing agility of some enormous people, and a strong desire to perform. He won a talent competition not for his excellent voice, but for cartwheeling into the orchestra pit to dodge the hook. The audience erupted in laughter.

Audiences erupted once more when they saw the moon-faced young man in A Noise from the Deep, a 1913 silent picture in which Arbuckle, soon to be known as "Fatty," had a pie thrown in his face. It was the first pie and the first face in Hollywood. Fatty could also pitch a pie with either hand and was accurate from 10 feet away. He joined Mack Sennett's slapstick comedy film team, alongside Charlie Chaplin, and he became a celebrity, one of the largest, with his compensation for a day on the set jumping from five dollars to a thousand, a huge sum at the time. In '21, he agreed to make twenty-two pictures for $3 million with Paramount Pictures Corporation.

"He was Falstaffian in size, if not in subtlety," the New York Times wrote. "His popularity was universal, particularly among children."

However, on September 5, 1921, during a Labor Day party in Fatty's suite at the Saint Francis Hotel in San Francisco, a very pretty twenty-five-year-old woman called Virginia Rappe fell ill and died four days later of peritonitis caused by a ruptured bladder. It appears possible that some of the Prohibition-era wine she drank during the party had been tainted. Methanol and other harmful additions were frequent in illicit alcohol.

"Fatty could not have caused her death," Dr. Al Oppenheim, the internist we mentioned earlier in relation to Tiger's junior golf career, adds. "Most likely, her chronic cystitis, exacerbated by bad alcohol, burst her bladder and caused the peritonitis that killed her."

Although the "evidence" against him appears comical today, and his chief accuser was fully discredited—and was, in fact, seeking to extort him—the case was pushed through by San Francisco District Attorney Murray's reckless ambition. Roscoe C. Arbuckle was arrested and charged with murder on September 10. The three-hundred-pound actor was accused of forcing himself on the poor woman and essentially crushing her. They put the huge man in a little room—Cell Number 12 in the San Francisco Hall of Justice, which one newspaper dubbed a "death cell." After eighteen days in jail, the grand jury indicted him for manslaughter.

Fatty's latest picture, Crazy to Marry, which was screening in cinemas across the country, was abruptly yanked.

The Fatty Arbuckle trials (there were three of them, resulting in two hung juries and an acquittal) were heaven-sent spectacles for the San Francisco Examiner and the other scandal-baiting Hearst newspaper. "Sold more newspapers than the sinking of the Lusitania," William Randolph Hearst was quoted as saying.

Few realised that Arbuckle would not accept certain defence testimony in the first two trials, even if it would have quickly ended the nonsense in his favour. Fatty was such a gentleman that he didn't want Miss Rapper's family to find out who their daughter actually was.

After five minutes of deliberation, the acquittal in March '22 came with an apology. But the harm had already been done. "Then came long years of Fatty Arbuckle's trial before public opinion," the New York Times stated in his obituary on June 30, 1933. "His rehabilitation efforts were entirely unsuccessful."

Arbuckle died of a heart attack in his sleep in 1933, at the age of 46.

Fatty was more wronged than wronged, yet the incident destroyed him. Tiger's outcome would be more complicated, because, like many of us, he was playing three hands of blackjack. He might go bankrupt in his personal life and endorsements, and he'd never be a SEAL, but the golf ball didn't know or care about what he did last night, and no one was kicking him out of tournaments because his presence ensured their success. Unlike Fatty, who was stigmatised even after his acquittal, Woods could still pursue what gave his life meaning. Tiger, on the other hand, could not request another take because he performed in front of a live crowd. Had he lost his following? If people are laughing in the wrong areas, no artist on a stage or between yellow nylon ropes can flourish.

Tiger returned to his happy zone, the practice tee, after the hiatus in Hattiesburg. Hank arrived in Orlando, and they began planning for the huge annual celebration in East Georgia. He worked on the massive sweeping hook he'd hit off the tee on thirteen, as well as the cut driver he'd hammered through the chute and up the hill on eighteen. Tiger's first competition after the Unpleasantness would be the Masters. He'd be prepared.

If the Masters would be ready for him was a different matter, thanks in part to the sanctimony of His Holiness William "Billy" Payne, Chairman of the Augusta National Golf Club, who used the dubious moral authority of his position to smear Tiger's nose in dirt.

Tiger played nine holes on the Sunday before tournament week, then marched to the rectory. He had a meeting with Himself. He kissed the ring, got down on one knee, went into the confessional— something. There isn't any video. Later, Rabbi Payne spoke.

"It is simply not the degree of his conduct that is so egregious here," he remarked in his annual media conference the day before the tournament started. "It's the fact that he disappointed all of us, especially our children and grandchildren." "Our hero failed to live up to the role model we saw for our children."

"Our hero" had broken up his family and lost his self-esteem, and everyone was mocking him, but he hadn't been through enough to satisfy devout Billy. How did Tiger avoid slugging him?

"Does there seem to be a way forward?" "I hope so," Imam Payne stated. "I believe there is. But, without a doubt, his future will be assessed not only by his performance versus par, but also by the sincerity of his efforts to improve."

We're not sure why Billy felt the need to take a shot from above at Tiger, and why he couldn't just keep his lips shut on the subject.

Can you imagine an official in any other sport being concerned about a player's "sincerity"? "We'd like to see better sincerity from Steph Curry this season," NBA commissioner Adam Silver will never say. Stealing—of bases and signs—is a part of the game of baseball. Even in the smallest of baseball leagues, mocking the opposing batters is prohibited. The multitudes of floppers in soccer brazenly display deception. Basketball coaches teach techniques for exaggerating contact in order to obtain a charging call (yell when you fall and slap the floor with both hands). Football players intentionally hold, trip, and clip, yet there is no punishment unless a zebra throws a flag. A running back speeding down the sideline with the ball will never stop to explain, "I stepped out of bounds back at the thirty-second mark." I'm sorry, I guess the back judge missed it." NFL Commissioner Roger Goodell is not without sanctimony of his own. Consider his remarks in the aftermath of the aforementioned Michael Vick and Ray Rice instances.

However, unless your name is Trump, golf's distinctive ethical culture necessitates self-policing. Golfers pass up numerous opportunities to cheat, and we call penalties on ourselves for infractions that no one else can see or know about. Sportsmanship is held up as the pinnacle of virtue. The eighteenth green ceremony, with handshakes and hats off, captures the essence quite nicely. No true golfer wants this tampered with. Tradition, sportsmanship, and honour are all admirable qualities.

Tiger turned the game's honour and shame into his personal life. What exactly did that mean? Anything?

"The game's conceit is that it or The First Tee teaches you how to behave," says John Strawn, author of Driving the Green, a golf industry executive. "What happens when golf's greatest player is exposed as a liar and a cheat?" That is why Billy Payne and others were so outspoken. Tiger's transgressions jeopardised all they hold dear."

Finally, the injured warrior enters the arena for some practice rounds. Augusta and Augusta National are packed; it's like 1997 all over again, and media attention is at an all-time high. Hard hooks and haymakers to the chest, head, and ego, we think the man has taken. But Tiger keeps his dignity and does his best in difficult circumstances.

He's playing alongside the most laid-back guy on the course, Fred Couples, who's being looked after by his similarly laid-back caddie, Joe LaCava. Tiger debuts a new look: wraparound sunglasses.

Tiger's extraordinary capacity to focus in the face of distraction is critical right now. He takes out his game face from his locker and puts it on. He blends focus, tranquillity, and clarity—perhaps with a little kale—and drinks it down. He's stepped up more than Bill Clinton ever did with his Apology. He'll play with his usual pride and flare because the people here adore him and, more importantly, understand him. Augusta National enthusiasts admire great genius in the golfing arts.

The tune-a-mint starts.

What? Do you remember if Tiger won or lost the 2010 Masters? He was defeated! It's a big deal. It was the worst competition anyone has ever attended. He had to say goodbye to his wife, his instructor, his caddie, and the Masters.

Tiger didn't "lose" the 2010 Masters in reverse order. In reality, he played really well, finishing in a tie for fourth place, five shots behind the winner, Phil Mickelson. For a man who hadn't competed in four months, that was an incredible performance.

But, since the huge, horrible story broke, Caddie Williams' relationship had deteriorated—significantly. Stevie was not involved in Tiger's extramarital activities, although most people assumed he was. The New Zealander, fed up with the press and being booed after winning a car race in Bay Park in the North Island city of Tauranga, had repeatedly begged the Team for a statement clearing him of any participation in the debacle. They told him no way. Absolving you would cast a negative light on the rest of the group.

Stevie got some things off his chest before resuming his grip on the Nike bag. On the way to the Orlando airport, from which they'd fly in Tiger's Gulfstream to Bush Field in Augusta, he expressed his outrage at being dragged into a scandal he'd had nothing to do with, how awful it had made his and his family's lives, how his calls had gone unanswered, and how the Team's indifference to his plight only fueled his rage. What about Tiger? Another change is that you will no longer spit at the hole when you miss a putt. And you're not going to just hurl your club in the direction of the golf bag after you're done, leaving your caddie to pick up the sticks off the ground, treating him as a servant rather than a partner.

Stevie desired an apology, increased respect, and improved communication. In addition, a raise.

The key message was that Williams didn't buy this sex addiction nonsense for a second. Tiger had simply been a pig who felt he could get away with it, in his opinion. Elin was a favourite of Stevie and his wife; Tiger, not so much lately.

"I had no sympathy for what he'd done," Williams wrote in his memoir. "I believe you have control over your actions, and I have no sympathy for people who become addicted to drugs, gambling, or sex." People make decisions, and he'd made this one.But I did sympathise with him for having to suffer in public when others might have sorted out their problems privately."

Williams' memories are coloured by the unpleasant way their relationship was going to end. He recalls a sadly diminished former hero whose comeuppance had arrived, rather than a fearless contender facing the music.

"I could immediately sense that the air around us had changed," Williams wrote. "The typical respectful and distant attitude toward Tiger was replaced by icy scorn. People all across the world, especially his adversaries, had lost respect for him and were no longer awestruck by him—his falsehoods and double life had been exposed. He was completely naked out there."

As Woods teed off for the opening round, a banner-pulling prop plane soared leisurely over the course. TIGER: DID YOU MEAN BOOTYISM? read the sign.

However, my attitude and energy improved. Apart from the banner, Stevie thought the build-up and the first two rounds were excellent. Tiger appeared more humble and appreciative, which was a breath of new air. However, after Tiger met with the press following his fantastic first two rounds—68 and 71—Williams was surprised to hear Steinie advise Tiger that in order to win, he needed to "stop being a nice guy" and return to his harsh old self. Williams was taken aback.

"[After] he had made a public commitment to a less snarling and aggressive Tiger, that he'd promised me to reform his bad habits, his main advisor was telling him the opposite," Williams would write.

"Right then, something inside of me shifted... My first reaction was, "I'm not going to be around for much longer."

But, really, should we care about this caddie's working conditions? There are at least two reasons why we shouldn't. For starters, Stevie had been generating around a million dollars every year for the past decade. Second, Tiger Woods was no insignificant golf pro. There were allowances for Beethoven, Einstein, Degas, and Ali. Was this genius unworthy? On the golf course, he wasn't a people person, and he'd never be approached to sell timeshares. He did various other things to compensate.

Another Team member felt the earth turn a day and a half after Steinie told Tiger to be harsh. "It suddenly hit me," Haney wrote. "I had a strong feeling that this would be my last time working for Tiger Woods."

Past slights and missed opportunities to say "thank you" had piled up like old newspapers by then, and in the tense atmosphere of the first tournament after the Revelations, everything felt bigger, louder, and more important. A new load of straw was thrown upon the camel's back. Some of Tiger's comments during the Saturday night press conference irritated Haney. "I don't have control of the ball," he said, adding that he had a "two-way miss" (his ball may go either right or left), which is poison for any golfer who wants to play well. Hank saw the remarks as direct jabs at himself, the swing's subcontractor.

Despite every imaginable hazard to his focus short of a hostage crisis, Tiger was only four strokes down after 54 holes. His competitiveness and laser beam focus were unparalleled.

However, the prospect of the final round did not excite him. Haney attempted and failed to say the right things to a grumpy student during the pre-game on the range. Finally, as Tiger walked away from the practice green toward the first tee, Hank tried "good luck." It would be their final words together.

Tiger had a wild up and down round that included a second shot hole-out on hole seven; his total was 69, which was very good but not good enough. Mickelson was victorious. CBS-TV's Peter Kostis guided the microphone to Tiger's mouth. This was one of those rare occasions when dipping a bucket into his vast well of clichés might be beneficial. For example, how fantastic it was to be back, how incredible the fan support had been, and how wonderful the weather had been. Instead, the grumpy warrior cavilled over his swing once more. In a phone call to Steinie that night, Haney quit.

Neither Haney nor Williams cite one evidence because of their client's negative attitude in their books. Didn't they get their news from the National Enquirer's website? For on Wednesday, the day before the Masters began, NE revealed another mistress story, but this one was different. The woman in question was a twenty-one-year-old college girl the Woodses had known since she was fourteen. Tiger had admitted to numerous flings, including liaisons with adult entertainers, but not this one. It appeared to be the final straw. Elin filed her paperwork. She was awarded custody of the children as well as almost $100 million.

So Tiger's decade in the wilderness began.

His personal life doesn't lend itself to data points—who doesn't?—but golf outcomes are essentially arithmetic, and his clearly followed a bell curve. After five years at the top, he lost his world number one ranking to Lee Westwood in October 2010. With his health and swing failing, he played only nine events in 2011, dropping his ranking to 52. The Tiger trajectory swooped drastically up when he won three times in 2012 and five more times in 2013—career totals for a very talented Tour player—but the abscissa and ordinate on his graph only revealed terrible news after that. He was growing elderly. He was getting less done. In 2015, his global ranking fell to 254.

Following Hank's departure at the end of that dreadful week in Augusta, Team Tiger needed to fill an essential position. A few months later, a GQ-looking man named Sean Foley auditioned for the job at the Team's rental house at Whistling Straits in Wisconsin during the PGA Championship. It's difficult to judge whether it was a tough or receptive crowd, because Tiger had just gone eighteen over in the previous tournament, the Bridgestone Invitational at Firestone, which he had won seven times. In any case, Foley was hired.

"Sean was super-convincing," Stevie said. "Even if his language was incomprehensible"—neural circuits, fascial links, and other such things. On the other hand, one of Foley's primary points was simple to understand. He told the boss to "lean into it." You're taking too many steps back.

Foley, a Canadian who lived and taught golf in Orlando, was around Tiger's age—both were in their mid-thirties. Perhaps a fellow Gen Xer would be a good collaborator. Hank was twenty years Tiger's senior, while Butch was thirty-two years older than his top student. Besides, Haney and Harmon weren't just old, they were old school, their basic thinking about golf instruction influenced by a 1957 book called Five Lessons.

Sean Foley was a different kettle of fish altogether.

First and foremost, he spoke biomechanics, not Hogan jargon. During his lessons, he employed video and a Doppler radar-based TrackMan. He was into rap music. His father is Scottish, and his mother is Guyana-born West Indian. Despite his lack of physical appearance, he had attended and played golf at Tennessee State, a historically black college. Foley was frequently rejected at TSU, possibly due to a lack of enough pigment. "So now when people ask me what it's like to be Tiger's coach and all those terrible things people say, I'm like, whatever," he told Charles McGrath of the New York Times. It doesn't disturb me in the least."

Tiger has no victories in 2010. Or for Williams, who saw them as his as well. The looper's relationship with the boss had degraded to business only after the Revelations and the Team's difficult handling of the aftermath in relation to the caddie. He was staring at the front door. And he walked, or was pushed, across it the following summer.

Stevie had given Adam Scott an impromptu pep talk shortly before the final round of the 2011 Masters, and the words of encouragement had propelled the tall Aussie to a 67 and a near-win. So when Tiger got hurt and couldn't compete in the next major, the US Open, Scott contacted and asked if Williams could be his bearer for the week. He answered sure, Tiger agreed, and the deal was done. Scott didn't make the cut.

It was the same scenario two weeks later, with Tiger still injured and unable to play, only this time there was an altercation. Stevie clarified that this was only a one-time occurrence and that he was not resigning. Tiger hesitantly agreed. He afterwards changed his mind. There were exchanges between the player, the caddie, and Steinie.

The last conversation went something like this: "If you caddie for Adam, we're done."

Then we're finished.

Another long-term romance ended. The bad blood was on display during the 2011 Bridgestone in Akron. Tiger finished last, with Fred Couples' ex, Joe LaCava, on the sack, and Scott won. Then the strangest thing happened: CBS-TV's David Feherty shoved the microphone up the caddie's nose. That never happens; Stevie was not prepared, and why should he be? He was too emotional, too focused on the now. "This is the greatest win of my career," he exclaimed, despite the fact that it wasn't even close.

When advance copies of The Big Miss hit the streets in early March 2012, Steinie's rage erupted, but he should have been angry at himself for failing to have Hank sign a nondisclosure agreement. The disclosures concerning Tiger's SEAL obsessions, as well as the popsicle, drew the most attention.

Meanwhile, Foley's high-tech training was bearing fruit. Although Tiger's uncharacteristically poor weekend rounds robbed him from winning three majors, and his 0-3-1 performance in the Ryder Cup did not please (Europe won), there were some bright spots. He won his first tournament in two years, the Arnold Palmer Invitational. By winning two more events, including Nicklaus' Memorial, the Marvellous Mr. Woods surpassed Jack in lifetime wins with 74. Another positive outcome had to be a tie for third place in the Open Championship at Royal Lytham, four shots behind the new Champion Golfer of the Year, Ernest Els.

He also met a female. Not any old gal. She was a magnificent Amazonian, a taller, more muscular Elin. She was Ms. Vonn, the world champion skier who had recently divorced her husband, also a skier.

Relationships involve competent give and take, as well as luck, magic, and some other unknown element, possibly astrology. Lindsey and Tiger may have checked every box, but they faced a fundamental barrier that few people face: their celebrity. They had little access to the kinds of normal activities that most of us may enjoy, such as bowling or stopping in for happy hour at Applebee's on a whim. Theirs was the low-oxygen altitude of high-profile dating, which necessitated an announcement when it began and another when it ended two and a half years later.

They appeared as a couple at the 2013 Masters, where an incident occurred that could be interpreted as a referendum on the former hero. Haters would find a new reason to hate; fans would have to keep pointing out that Tiger wasn't just trying to hide an offence, but he also didn't complain when he received a two-shot penalty on top of a one-shot penalty. He ended up with an eight, a human hair away from an eagle three on fifteen. It was possible that it cost him the tournament.

You may recall Tiger hitting a fantastic third shot on the fifteenth in the second round, which became perfectly horrible. This wedge was so accurate that the ball landed on the bottom of the pin and bounced into the pond in front of the green. And the audience grumbled. Bummer!

What happens next? Tiger had three alternatives for getting the ball back into play, each of which cost a one-shot penalty: Play from a spray-painted circle near the pond; pinpoint the spot where the water ball caused a ripple, line it up with the pin, and hit a ball along that vector from as far back as he desired; or play from the initial spot again. Tiger chose choice three, but he made a mistake. He backed up a few yards, dropped a new pelota from shoulder height, struck a magnificent shot, and sunk the short putt for a bogey six instead of playing from the original place. That should have been an eight, with a two-shot penalty for the wrong drop. As a result, the scorecard he signed was wrong. This necessitates disqualification. This was not done because the next morning, Masters officials invoked a new regulation, 33-7, that allowed fines to be levied after the event in "extraordinary circumstances."

Were these situations unusual enough? A commotion erupted, almost drowning out the competition. Let's move on from this innocuous error, wrote Thomas Boswell in the Washington Post. Not so fast, says The Golf Channel's Brandel Chamblee: "It is his responsibility to disqualify himself." Anything less is simply unacceptable."

Tiger chose Boswell. He could have avoided being helped into a green jacket with an asterisk on the breast pocket if he had gone Chamblee. And that would have been a PR coup for a person who desperately needed one. "Reasonable people have questioned the legitimacy of my score," he may have responded. "I have decided to withdraw in order to put an end to the controversy." I'm not going to place myself above the game."

In any case, he played. I tied for fourth place. Adam Scott was victorious. Stevie plucked the cloth off the stick on eighteen, as is the right of the winning caddy, adding to his collection of captured battle flags.

Then there's the Achilles tendon, the lumbar disc, the wrist, the elbow, the neck, and the medial collateral ligament. Sciatica, muscle spasms, and shooting pain are all symptoms of sciatica.

Rep the following: Achilles tendon, lumbar disc, wrist, elbow, and medial collateral ligament. Sciatica, muscle spasms, and shooting pain are all symptoms of sciatica.

Tiger's painful bodily parts resulted in numerous withdrawals and DESs (Didn't Even Start) towards the end of 2013 and beyond. Finally, it led to surgery on his spine, which used to symbolise a permanent "I'm just going to watch the game on TV" time off for an athlete but no longer does. A microdiscectomy for a surgeon is similar to an oil change for a car mechanic thanks to the use of a marvellous equipment known as an endoscope. Perhaps a valve replacement is a better analogy: removing bone from the back to free up a nerve is a dangerous procedure with potentially disastrous effects.

But Tiger had fantastic surgeons, and each of his several "procedures" was declared a success, at least in post-op. He had his first microdiscectomy in March 2014, his second in September 2015, and his third just a month after to "relieve discomfort." His pain may have been relieved (on some days), but his golf...

Butch Harmon was asked about his former student in April 2016. "I don't know if Tiger can ever come back," he remarked. "Oh, God, I hope so." It would be fantastic for the game. But Tiger will not accept mediocrity."

But he did it. He was poor at best. It was as if someone had put on his swooshes and stepped into his shoes. Someone who resembled Tiger shot 82 in Phoenix and 85 at the Memorial; this same person suffered from the chip yips, golf's second most amusing ailment. Only chronic shanks cause more restrained laughter. Unless, of course, you're the yipper or the shanker, in which case you want to kill yourself.

MBE Sir Nick Faldo, thrice a Masters winner, shared a sorrowful comment from Tiger at the Masters Champions dinner two years prior on "The Dan Patrick Show" in August '18. Tiger claimed that his three back procedures had all failed. "'I'm done, my back is done,' he said quietly. "I'm not going to play golf again," Nick declared. "He was in anguish, he was in torment... He was unable to move."

Tiger attempted a riskier, more intrusive procedure in April 2017 with the stated goal of living a normal life: spinal fusion. It's not an unusual procedure; poor baby boomer backs are one of the major reasons for the roughly 600,000 disc fusions performed in the United States every year. Why do 600,000 people do it? To alleviate discomfort. What do they receive? Stability comes at the expense of flexibility. As for the discomfort...

According to a research cited by Gina Kolata in the New York Times, approximately half of those undergoing lumbar (lower) spine fusions utilised opioids to help manage pain. Nine percent of patients discontinued taking Vicodin or other pain relievers after surgery. However, 13% of those who had never used opioids previously became long-term users.

Tiger was among the largest group of those who used before and after.

"It's difficult to define success," Kolata wrote. "By [one] definition—more than thirty percent pain relief and thirty percent improvement in function—only about half of fusion operations succeed."

Tiger's Anterior Lumbar Interbody Fusion was performed in mid-April 2017 by Dr. Richard Guyer of the Center for Disc Replacement at the Texas Back Institute in Plano, Texas. Dr. Guyer removed the lower disc in the patient's back and replaced it with a metal cage packed with bone obtained from a cadaver or the patient's hip. Due to doctor-patient confidentiality, specifics were withheld. As is customary, everyone hailed the operation a success—presumably because no one died. It would be months before it was apparent whether the procedure had been worthwhile. Meanwhile, Tiger's constant companion would be suffering.

It became too much after about a month. You may have heard that on May 29, 2017, around two a.m., deputies from the Palm Beach County Sheriff's Department discovered Tiger sleeping at the wheel on the side of the road fifteen miles from his home. The drowsy man was invited to exit the vehicle. He was dressed casually in cargo shorts, a Nike tee, and untied sneakers. The cops cuffed him after he failed the field sobriety test, which may be regular operating procedure but seems absurd considering the prisoner's state. At the station, they took a mug shot, and then it was to state your name, height, weight, hair colour, and eye colour, blow into this tube, seat over there, and do you want a lawyer.

We don't have to speculate on Tiger's state of mind. On that front, the tox screen excels. He was in discomfort and had taken Dilaudid (hydromorphone) and Vicodin (hydrocodone) to relieve it. His mood was deteriorating; he was also taking Xanax and THC, the psychoactive component of marijuana. And because he couldn't sleep due to pain, worry, or melancholy, he had taken Ambien.

Two opiates, two sedatives, and THC made for a lethal drug cocktail. Accidental overdose deaths are on the rise in the United States—an amazing and heartbreaking 70,237 occurred in 2017—and are the biggest cause of death for Americans under the age of fifty. In 2017, there were slightly more than 40,000 traffic deaths on American highways. If Tiger had perished that night in a car accident, someone would have to decide which category he belonged in.

"I feel like [it was] a massive scream for help," swimmer Michael Phelps, who had been treated for addiction, said. He became friends with Tiger.

The next day's widely circulated headline, "DUI of the Tiger," was smart but not really amusing. Because the majority of us have been personally or indirectly affected by an overdose fatality. And most of us recognized a man at rock bottom because we've been there, or almost so.

Hogan, Silton, Alexander, Peete, and Sifford were respectively driven over by a bus, shot through the head, charred to toast in an aircraft crash, deprived, deformed, and rejected. These golfers accomplished amazing things despite the obstacles thrown in their path by fate, and their stories inspire us. In contrast, we briefly considered Arbuckle, who suffered but did not persist.

But, before we hum "Eye of the Tiger" and see a film montage of sweat, anguish, and sacrifice leading up to Tiger's dramatic return to the mountaintop, consider one more comeback story. Perhaps hers was the finest of all.

Mildred Ella "Babe" Didrikson Zaharias' celebrity is difficult to overestimate today. The lantern-jawed Norwegian immigrant's daughter was as large as Tiger and was to women's sports what Secretariat was to horse racing. She, like Tiger, captured the attention of the world as a teenager when she was the top player on the best basketball team in the country. She launched a baseball 300 feet into the air. She took first place in the sewing category at the South Texas State Fair. She won the AAU national track and field championship in 1932 all by herself. When you enter eight events, win five of them, and tie for first in the sixth, you don't need teammates. A month later, in the Los Angeles Olympics, she established three world records in three different events: the 80-metre hurdles, the high jump, and the javelin. On a technicality, two golds and one silver.

In some ways, Babe was the anti-Tiger, a generalist genius who could do a variety of things exceedingly well. Tiger had been a specialist since he was a baby, never dabbling in quoits, sewing, or anything else until he discovered the aquatic realm as a diver in 2003.

Following the Olympics, the twenty-one-year-old greatest female athlete on the planet played eighteen holes for the first time, shooting about 100. But she enjoyed it. She dominated her new game three years later, winning fourteen amateur events in a row at one time. Miss Didrikson was capable of beating boys. She qualified for four PGA Tour events, but was not invited, and made the 36-hole cut in three of them. Annika Sorenstam performed admirably at The Colonial in 2003, but her 145 did not qualify her for the weekend. Babe is the only woman to have made a cut in the men's league in the United States (Michelle Wie once made a cut in an Asian men's competition, the SK Telecom Open).

The Babe missed one of four cuts, at the 1938 Los Angeles Open, when she was paired with and distracted by a friendly bear of a man named George Zaharias, a professional wrestler and kindred soul. Within a year, they were married. When there were notebooks out, Big George—who played a bad guy in wrestling's jock opera—exaggerated his wife's accomplishments, and Babe played along.

Oh, the minds she shattered. She had no trace of the shyness gene. She ate more harm than a prize pig. In his book Wonder Girl, biographer Don Van Natta portrays the story brilliantly.

She co-founded the LPGA with a small group of other women in 1950. Everyone knew who the celebrity was. Shirley Spork, a fellow pro, recalled her pal approaching any group in the locker room or on the practice tee and saying, "Well, the Babe's here." Who will come in second? "Perhaps you, Louise?"

Louise Suggs, one of the finest female golfers of all time, despised Babe. I despised her. Others in the game said that the Babe's muscled shoulders were too square, her walk and attitude were too masculine, and that despite her marriage to Mr. Zaharias, she was sleeping with Miss Dodd, referring to fellow LPGAer Betty Dodd. Babe didn't merely flout athletic feminine rules; she ground them under her heel and yelled, screw you. When she felt too hot in front of a large crowd, she just squirted out of her half-slip. Shocking!

She wasn't exactly Miss Sportsmanship. "I don't think I've ever seen anyone take losing less gracefully," Betsy Rawls said of her old opponent. Fans, though, admired her as much as they did Arnie and, subsequently, Tiger.

In 1953, colon cancer struck. The disease was much more deadly back then than it is now, and it was also a forbidden subject. Babe, on the other hand, lamented in secret. She utilised her platform to persuade people to be tested for God's sake, and she undoubtedly saved several lives.

She had an -ectomy as well as an -ostomy. The press covered her rehabilitation in the same frenzied manner as it had four years earlier, when she was known as America's Patient: "BABE WALKS, EATS SOLID FOOD" and "BABE TAKES RIDE, NOW FEELS BETTER" were typical all-caps headlines.

Her energy began to dwindle, but she would not die at home with George. She teed it up in Chicago four months after her cancer surgery and finished third.

Ed Sullivan's representatives called. Will the Babe be on the show? When your television only had three or four channels, watching Ed Sullivan's Sunday night variety program was a national tradition. Yes, Babe would be delighted to appear. But she wouldn't just show up; she'd perform. So, after the cadaverous host introduced his athletic guest, said guest said, "Thanks for all the cards and letters" and then produced her M. Hohner Marine Band Model #1896 harmonica and blew out a peppy version of "Begin the Beguine " in the key of C, complete with wah-wah and tremolo effects produced with her right hand. Ed requested an encore. Miss Betty Dodd, Babe's pupil, appeared on stage with her guitar and they performed "Little Train A-Chugging'."

The golfers/musicians travelled from New York to Chicago to record a single for Mercury (A-side: "I Felt a Little Teardrop"). "Detour" is the B-side). The next day, United Press International announced, "BABE BEGINS HILL-BILLY MUSIC CAREER."

Babe won all of her early 1954 events, but she was like a clock ticking away. She went to Boston for the Big One that summer. Mrs. Zaharias stormed to a large lead after two rounds at Salem Country Club, thanks in large part to Betty's nursing assistance. However, both the men's and women's US Opens required a 36-hole finish. Does this sound familiar? Was she on par with Skip Alexander and Ben Hogan?

Well... hell, sure! Babe bogeyed a few holes at the end, but she completed. And she won by a score of twelve. She performed a little shimmy as her putt from eighteen feet to win by thirteen inches just missed, and her adoring gallery stood and shouted. She had to be tired, but she didn't show it.

"Just eighteen months after a cancer operation," remarked the newsreel's booming voice. "Here she is, a clear winner. "One of sports history's most inspiring comebacks!"

Mrs. Zaharias' cancer reappeared soon after the 1954 US Open, assuming it had ever left. She withered away. Betty Dodd and her guitar were Babe's constant friends for more than a year and a half when she was mostly bedridden. "George wasn't there 90% of the time she was in the hospital." "He didn't want to mess with it," Betty explained to me in 1990. "I used to be a player for her. The majority of the songs are ballads. I wasn't sure I wanted to play."

In an attempt to relieve her anguish, physicians cut her spine at the end. Babe said, "I just want to see a golf course one last time," on what everyone knew would be her final Christmas with her longtime friends, the Bowens, in Fort Worth.

The Bowens' yacht-like Cadillac rolled through a Colonial Country Club side gate and came to a halt on a maintenance lane. Babe stepped out of the car and staggered up the little incline to the second green. She bowed her head. The dying star ran her hands back and forth across the grass for a few long moments.

CHAPTER 3

FIRE AT IT

Sunday, April 7

"Almost miraculous."

This week's words are "usually" and "always." As in "I always eat at Rae's Coastal Cafe on Tuesday nights and I usually have the shrimp pâté and jerk chicken" or "they always put the pin front left on number six on Sunday" or "we always rent the same house at Jones Creek every year" and "we always get drunk on Jameson whiskey at the Irish Tourist Irish Board party." Rituals are an important part of the fun at the only one of golf's four majors that is held in the same location year after year.

People enjoy masters' rituals. When people are happy, they drink one more drink than when they are sad. They order larger steaks, deliver better jokes, and make better friends—all of which becomes part of the ritual.

My usual routine calls for a Tuesday arrival to prepare for the big Wednesday game in Waynesboro, a small town in Burke County that promotes itself as "The Bird Dog Capital of the World." Waynesboro Country Club, on the other hand, is no dog, and it takes great satisfaction in not gouging your eyes out during Masters Week, unlike almost every other golf course and hotel in the Central Savannah River Area. Twenty-five dollars gets you eighteen holes and a cart. Beer is only $1.50 a can and is served cold. Please give me 10.

Tat Thompson, a former Augusta banker and an energetic and skilled first tee debater, is the first communicator in Waynesboro. He paces the grassy platform like an excited Baptist preacher on a scorching Sunday morning on this special day. "No, no, no, that's not gonna work!" exclaims Tat. His Georgia accent is thick enough to cut and spread on toast. "I'd like Mully, Danny, and Tim." A man costs ten dollahs. There are no holes. Lauderdale is a four-man team. "What do you think, Baggah?"

For unknown reasons, I am "Bagger Vance" to Tat, whose outmatched negotiators include Danny Fitzgerald, Tim Wright, the Ash and Hopkins brothers, Mike Rucker, Doc Coleman, Brian Leonard, Walt the Pharmacist, and a slew of other colourful and budget-conscious characters. Depending on how drunk we are, we sometimes head to Tat's house for an after-golf game of Termite, which is three-card guts.

"A tradition unlike any other," Jim Nantz adds, although he might omit the A and replace it with a s to give a more authentic sense of the region. From the glory game at Waynesboro to the flabby egg salad and pimento cheese sandwiches you always get at the concession booth to the right of thirteen to the holiest of holies, the Champions Dinner on Tuesday night, it's all part of the package. A couple of beloved old pros usually get the affair started by whacking off a tee ball in the chill of first light on Thursday morning, and they always will. (And don't you just adore how hard Gary Player works on his one shot of the day?)

TV, too. For those of us who watch from the couch, which is the vast majority of us, hearing the same CBS voices year after year is critical. Unless there is thundering commentary from Henry Longhurst, Ben Wright, and now Verne Lundquist, the sixteenth hole is just a short shot over a shallow pond. Pat Summerall hosted the show from 1968 until Nantz took over 20 years later. Both were and are excellent, but two anchors in fifty years? Thank you very much for the change.

Tiger, who has played in twenty-one of them, surely has his own Masters rituals, which include winning (four times) or finishing in the top ten (nine other times).

He generally arrives on Monday of tournament week, but Caddie LaCava persuaded the boss to come in a day early this year so he could adjust to the speed of the greens.

It was a short journey. Tiger's gorgeous sixteen-passenger Gulfstream G550 flew the 500 miles from Palm Beach to Augusta Regional Airport in about an hour. Adam Scott, another model rocket ship owner, stationed his at Daniel Field, Augusta's close-in private strip. Within days, the small airport would be crammed with corporate planes worth hundreds of millions of dollars. The G550 alone costs around $42 million.

Tiger and Joey met at the National with the two Woods kids, new girlfriend Ms. Erica Herman, the family dog, and possibly some more ensconced at a gorgeous riverfront rental house in North Augusta. With eighty young contestants in the Drive, Chip, Putt competition, as well as their parents, friends, and spectators, it was a packed place. The Golf Channel highlighted the feel-good tournament, which featured nine-year-old Angela Zhang of Bellevue, Washington, a seventy-five-pounder who won her age group with a 189-yard drive. Former Masters champions, including the defending champion, Patrick Reed, handed out trophies and posed for pictures. Scott, Bubba Watson, Nick Faldo MBE, Mark O'Meara, Bernhard Langer, and Mike Weir were among the other green jackets executing the grip and grin.

Woods, on the other hand, would not be waiting with the other champions; he would be working. He also had a secret.

"I told Joey I'd been grinding my butt off at home," Tiger revealed in an intriguing interview with GolfTV's Henni Zuel. "And I said,'I'm not playing today, but I'll chip and putt.'"

On the first nine greens, he "just worked on speed" and the unusually huge amount of breaks in Augusta National greens.

During this time, he apparently told his looper about the secret he'd discovered in the mud on the practice tee in Florida: "a swing in which I could start drawing the ball." I've lost some of my fastball velocity because I don't have the length I used to have. As a result, I must rely on my driver. And I discovered that I could hit a draw with [any club] while still being able to hit a slider... "So I was like, OK, we've got something here."

Tiger had discovered his innate talent to hit and control a right to left curveball, also known as a draw. The draw and its bothersome big brother, the hook, are good to have in your quiver at Augusta National's left-bending holes, which include but are not limited to holes two, nine, ten, and thirteen. Furthermore, hooks and draws get off to a fast start, making them a helpful, if risky, approach for anyone looking for more distance off the tee. The "slider" Tiger mentioned is a safety shot, a defensive left-to-right spinner that doesn't travel as far as a draw but is usually easy to spot. A fading is another term for it.

That Tiger would be excited about ball flight did not appear to be in the cards when we last saw him, in May of '17, when he was drowsy and disoriented and under arrest in the middle of the night at the Palm Beach County Sheriff's Department. But he went on to accomplish what he needed to do after that. He checked himself into a drug rehab centre and graduated. I entered a guilty plea to reckless driving. I completed my fifty hours of community service. although I'm not sure how. Entered and completed a DUI first-offender program.

What about the back? Well . . .

"It's almost miraculous," Jack Zigler, president of the International Society for the Advancement of Spinal Surgery, told Washington Post reporter Adam Kilgore. "On the one hand, you have someone who is in excellent physical condition and is extremely motivated—the ideal patient." On the other side, he's returning to an incredible degree of function. The chances of you ever returning there are slim."

The surgeon, 21st-century medical technology, and the patient deserve credit. Tiger did not have to combat the tendency of most back patients to move extremely slowly, if at all, given his enthusiasm for rigorous work and workouts. Instead, he rehabbed as if his golf career was at stake, which it was. He was a man without a backup plan, making him extremely dangerous. Then, in 2018, he won the Tour Championship.

While Tiger and Joe skipped from green to green on that glorious Sunday afternoon, Brooks Koepka, another Nike-wearing early arrival, slugged balls on the practice range.

Seven months previously, Woods and Koepka were featured in the same headline. They finished one-two at the 2018 PGA Championship at Bellerive in St. Louis, with Brooks first and Tiger second by two strokes. They utterly torched the course; in the second round, on the final green, Brooks hit the lip with a putt for a 62, the lowest score ever shot in a major. Tiger's final-round tee shots flitted around like a bug in a car, but he made every putt and finished with a score of 64.

"Woods, who in his youthful pomp was accustomed to obliterating courses and fields in the manner now the domain of Koepka, nodded in approval," wrote Ewan Murray in the Guardian.

"'He's driving it 330 yards down the fairway,' remarked [Tiger]. 'He's got nine irons for approach shots when most of us are hitting five or four irons, and he's putting brilliantly. That adds up to a significant lead."

Exactly. With victories in the 2017 and 2018 US Opens, as well as the '18 and '19 PGAs, could Brooks be the next Intimidator? Could Tiger be scared of the soon-to-be world number one? That has never happened before. Ewan Murray has this to say about Koepka's uncommon calm: "The 28-year-old makes great play of the fact that golf does not excite him, which makes one wonder what on earth he would achieve if reinvigorated."

But there is no simmering rivalry between these Florida neighbours; there is no purposeful psychological warfare. "Other than me and my team, everybody was rooting for Tiger—as they should," Koepka said from the Bellerive winner's circle. "He's the greatest player to ever play the game, and to have the comeback he's having is just incredible." Not exactly combative language.

There is no purposeful psychological warfare... but who can deny that Koepka scares the hell out of his contemporaries with his physical appearance, play, and exploding stardom? He separates himself. Koepka came at the range on Wednesday at the AT&T Byron Nelson Invitational in May, a month after the Masters, surrounded by a phalanx of support staff: one caddie, two agents, and three other individuals who could have been an instructor, a physio, and a Nike person (or maybe a cook; I know he has a cook). Despite the fact that the Trinity Forest Golf Club practice tee is over a hundred yards wide and not overly crowded, Team Koepka parked over to the side, not even on the tee, and Brooks shot balls diagonally at the target greens in the centre. After finishing his practice session, the broad-shouldered pro and his crew reformed their armada and sailed toward the exit. My deadline was approaching. It was time to be impolite. I intruded on their personal space. They accelerated their pace. I introduced myself, asked Brooks if we could talk at his leisure, and offered him a copy of The Masters. I joked that it would be ideal for a sleepless night.

"Thank you," he murmured, handing the paperback to his agent as if it were a Shake 'n Bake coupon. To put it another way, swiftly.

"Not a reader, eh, Brooks?" Giving up, I said.

"I read!" he said, then he was gone.

Monday, April 8

"His Own Self"

Because of where they'd been and the ideas they'd had a month before, Jerry Tarde and Michael O'Malley and the others in the Golf Digest house were in for a long week. They took flights from Kennedy or LaGuardia to DFW, leased cars, and drove to a white stone cathedral in downtown Fort Worth. They heard and delivered brief statements, stared blankly into space, and listened to the ceremony's walkout music: "We'll Meet Again," an upbeat World War II hymn by a toothy English pop singer named Vera Lynn. The music was chosen by Dan Jenkins. Jenkins, the Thomas A. Edison of modern sports writing and the heart and soul of Sports Illustrated, Golf Digest, and countless novels, died on March 7. He was ninety years old.

"I grew up reading Dan Jenkins," Tarde, the editor-in-chief, told the gathering. "It shaped my life."

"I worked as Dan's editor. It had been a 23-year collaboration. When it was his turn, Executive Editor O'Malley said, "It didn't feel like a job." "He'd make you laugh and think at the same time."

Tarde and O'Malley, together with their writers and staff, would continue because that's what you do, but... the Masters without Jenkins? It would not be the same. It wasn't going to be the same. Not only did Dan deliver content that made everyone proud and tell a narrative that made everyone laugh, but he was also a court holder and an organiser of fun that you never wanted to end.

"There was something called the Jenkins Races," Tarde said. "Around 9:30 p.m., someone would bring in the pairing sheets for the next day. A table would seat seven or eight men. Dan would say, 'OK, low pair,' and we'd place our wagers. Alternatively, high foreigner, low guy, high couple. Dan was the commissioner, and he'd appoint a secretary to keep things organised. Frank Hannigan [a USGA high priest who is also a delightful and hilarious man] would call in. We'd all forget who we'd gambled on by then. It was one of the week's best social gatherings."

Jenkins moderated another table on the second level of the Augusta National clubhouse for over thirty years. A diverse group of golf and literary titans toasted the night and tackled the big concerns. As a counterbalance to the eloquently profane golf writer for the Pittsburgh Press, I'd choose the simply eloquent: Tom Brokaw, George Plimpton, Dave Marr, Ben Crenshaw, Herbert Warren Wind, Summerall, and Nantz. And, of course, Dan. "Players are dumber today," he would say to get the conversation started. Alternatively, "the LPGA needs shorter shorts."

Jenkins covered the Masters 68 times (in person, of course). He enjoyed the event enough to criticise it, such as when its organisers were stupid enough to allow the greens to go soft. In truth, despite his sharp, mordant humour, he adored golf, golf tournaments, and players, but he held just one man in high regard: his Fort Worth hometown hero, Ben Hogan. Dan was Ben's tireless supporter and protector. "Ben Hogan worked harder, overcame more, and achieved more than just about any athlete you can name," Jenkins wrote in a blurb for my 1996 biography, Hogan. "I was privileged to cover many of his most thrilling victories, and that remains one of my most treasured memories from a lifetime of sports writing."

Dan became Palmer's confidante as Hogan faded. Dan and Nicklaus got close when Arnie's star faded. Jack had lost his sparkle, and Tiger... wouldn't say anything. Despite the fact that both Jenkins and Woods were paid by Golf Digest, Tiger rebuffed every request for an interview with the Dean of American Sportswriters. Jenkins was present for all fourteen of Tiger's key victories, so it would have been simple. For example, during the 2006 Open Championship at Royal Liverpool, Hank Haney and Jenkins both stayed in the magazine's rented property. Tiger dropped his teacher off at the house every week after their post-round practice session, but he refused invites to come inside for a beer, a conversation, or a game of darts. As you may recall, he won that week.

"We have nothing to gain" from meeting with Jenkins, Steinie remarked, a short-sighted attitude that did not serve his client well, because there were times when Tiger could have used an influential media friend. Perhaps the Team was afraid of a give-and-take or a perjury trap with the quick-witted writer. The standoff upset Dan, so he shone a bright light on the immortals. That Team Tiger would not allow this added acid to the ink in an essay headlined "Nice (Not) Knowing You" for the February 2010 issue of Golf Digest, published a few months after the fall. Here are two of the gentler passages:

"I'll tell you what Hogan, Palmer, and Nicklaus were like when they were at their peak," Jenkins wrote. "They were just as popular as Tiger, and they faced similar demands on their time, but they handled it with grace, and often with ease and enjoyment."They were never what Tiger had always permitted himself to be: spoiled, pampered, concealed, guarded, choreographed, and entitled." Jenkins addressed his annoyance with his forced separation from the only great golfer since Harry Vardon that he never interviewed four years later by clicking out another write-around on his Olympia (a write-around, as you may recall, is a story or book executed without the cooperation of its subject; and an Olympia is a typewriter, an ancient mechanical device). The well-known "My (Fake) Interview With Tiger":

Q. Why now?

A. Steinie says I have to rebuild my brand.

Q. Why? TV still loves you. The print press still loves you. The average fans still love you. Of course, the average fans still love the Kardashians, too, but I feel sure America will find a cure for this someday.

A. I just do what Steinie says.

Q. Why haven't you fired Steinie, by the way? You've fired everyone else. Three gurus, Butch, Hank, and Sean Foley. Two caddies, Fluff and Stevie. Your first agent, Hughes Norton, who made you rich before you'd won anything. Other minions.

A. I'll probably get around to it. I like to fire people. It gives me something to do when I'm not shaping my shots.

Q. Who would you rather run over in a car first, Brandel Chamblee or me?

A. Who's Brandel Chamblee? How many majors has he won? How many has he even played?

"We have nothing to gain" from meeting with Jenkins, Steinie remarked, a short-sighted attitude that did not serve his client well, because there were times when Tiger could have used an influential media friend. Perhaps the Team was afraid of a give-and-take or a perjury trap with the quick-witted writer. The standoff upset Dan, so he shone a bright light on the immortals. That Team Tiger would not allow this added acid to the ink in an essay headlined "Nice (Not) Knowing You" for the February 2010 issue of Golf Digest, published a few months after the fall. Here are two of the gentler passages:

"I'll tell you what Hogan, Palmer, and Nicklaus were like when they were at their peak," Jenkins wrote. "They were just as popular as Tiger, and they faced similar demands on their time, but they handled it with grace, and often with ease and enjoyment."They were never what Tiger had always permitted himself to be: spoiled, pampered, concealed, guarded, choreographed, and entitled."

Jenkins addressed his annoyance with his forced separation from the only great golfer since Harry Vardon that he never interviewed four years later by clicking out another write-around on his Olympia (a write-around, as you may recall, is a story or book executed without the cooperation of its subject; and an Olympia is a typewriter, an ancient mechanical device). The well-known "My (Fake) Interview With Tiger":

Patrick Reed couldn't believe how good he felt as king. "It was awesome," the 2018 Masters champion remarked of his return to the scene of his rise. "I hadn't been back all year until Sunday," when, as previously stated, he provided the kids a delight just by being there at the Drive, Pitch, Putt competition. "Everyone was saying, 'Hey, Champ!' and my caddie got bib number one." Then on Wednesday, I'll host the dinner. Ray Floyd, Gary, Jack, Mr. Watson, and so on..."

Mr. Watson is not Bubba, but Tom. Although Bubba was also present.

Reed went to Augusta State University, which has since been renamed Augusta University and is located only down Berckmans Road and then to the left on Walton Way from the National. The bright, exceptionally hard working, and determined young man led the Jaguars to two NCAA championships, but he received little support from his hometown fans when winning the Masters. That's terrible!

"The feeling around the eighteenth green when he won was subdued to the point of being awkward," Alan Shipnuck of GOLF Magazine recalled a year ago. Because the estrangement from Reed's parents, who live in Augusta, culminated in a Montague and Capulet melodrama, popular opinion was on the side of mom and dad rather than the in-laws. But I didn't want to bring it up in our brief conversation, and I sensed or believed Reed was pleased to avoid the subject.

"The most difficult shots on the back nine, of course." If you lay up, the wedge is fifteen. And the tee ball on hole number eighteen. You're emerging through a chute. It's easier with a strong wind since you can simply aim for the bunker... "Until my last three or four rounds, I tried drawing the ball (his natural spin) off that tee."

Reed's block-out swing is an entertaining club-twirling contortion he makes to avoid hooks. It's similar to Tiger's slider, but funnier.

I thanked Patrick and wished him luck. The poor guy has taken a beating for his occasionally off-putting earnestness, the family situation, and for daring to imitate you-know-who's Sunday outfit of red shirt and black slacks. I'm not sure if it's an homage or an insult; hopefully the latter.

Tiger looked great in dove grey Nike Men's Flat Front Flex Pants and a thought-provoking inky blue Nike TW Vapour Mock Polo on this grey Monday morning, six days before he and Reed would face the world in their competing red and black suits. Justin Thomas and Fred Couples accompanied him out early, wearing who cares. Tiger's clothes were important because of apparel scripting, which is Nike letting shops all over the world know ahead of time what Woods will wear each day—at least for tournament rounds—so they could stock up. A new look was, of course, just a click away for internet consumers. The shirts for the competition would be navy, grey, lilac, and fire engine red. Only $85 each piece.

And this was clever: Nike had pushed Nike's manufacturer to recreate an image of two prayer hands, one in a golf glove, within Tiger's Air Zoom TW71 sneakers, just where the heels rest. It was a witty reference to Amen Corner, the challenging three-hole stretch that begins the back nine at Augusta National. As in: I hope I get three pars. Amen.

Tiger, Justin, and Fred shot up on the par three sixteenth, then walked to the front of the tee, dropped another ball, and drew out their lowest lofted irons in response to passionate pleas from the property's largest and happiest throng. On the count of three, the trio simultaneously skipped shots off the pond's surface, up toward, and even onto the green: another crowd favourite and tradition.

And the fans—sorry, patrons—clapped and hollered as they marched along, looking up at the sky and saying, "Do not rain." Because their tickets were not inexpensive. Those who ordered early in the year spent around $450 for Monday and $750 on Tuesday. Wednesday tickets were more expensive since another popular event, the Par 3 competition, takes place in the afternoon. For Wednesday, set aside $1,500. Prices increased as the deadline approached.

"Demand was about the same, maybe a little up from last year," says Clyde Pilcher, who practically pioneered the Masters ticket resale market and is still one of the game's top players. "This year's Tuesday price was $100 higher..." Badges [valid Monday through Sunday] ranged from $5,000 to $6,500.Nowadays, everything is corporate. Because badges are so expensive, few mom and pop shops purchase them."

Pilcher, 67, was a poorer-than-poor Augusta native whose all-encompassing work ethic made high school attendance an inconvenient impediment to acquiring money. Richmond Academy Assistant Principal Duford noticed that because of all his absences, Clyde might get straight A's for the rest of his life and still not graduate. OK, see you later, said the go-getter, who lacked a certificate. He went to work, doing two jobs at once. The City of Augusta Water Works Department, Crane's Menswear, Borden's Ice Cream, three separate gas stations, and Roto-Rooter were among his employees. This last posting was crucial because it spurred him to strike out on his own. Pilcher founded Budget Sewer Company with a 1961 Chevy C-10 pickup truck and a dream. His big break was the enormous butter spill at the Murray Biscuit Company, which his competitors didn't want to meddle with and which Pilcher fixed by cutting the handle off a shovel and digging himself down deep into the clogged drain. Budget Sewer quickly lived up to their tagline, "We're #1 in #2."

And how did this lead to his Masters ticket business?

"In '77 or '78, I was pumping' out Mrs. Daisy Gallegos's septic tank at 301 Berckmans Road," a small property across the street from Augusta National's Gate 6. "And she said she didn't want to mess around with that house any longer." 'How much do you want?' I inquired. She answers, '$36,700.' 'I'll take it,' I responded.

Mrs. Clyde Pilcher questioned the purchase, but Clyde calculated that parking automobiles would earn enough money to meet six of the $243.41 house payments to the mortgagor, the Bank of Texas.

"We got $2 a car, fifty cars at a time," Clyde says; when his neighbour's competition hired a cheerleader to entice clients, he got an even cuter cheerleader: his seven-year-old daughter, Traci. He simply escorted her to the curb and handed her Richmond Academy purple pom-poms. That's all there is to it, honey, shake 'em! And, while parking costs increased over time, from two to five to ten to twenty dollars per car, a new revenue stream quickly surpassed them.

Pilcher's property was the ideal location for connecting customers with what they desired the most. If a badge or a ticket were to be exchanged, there was no need for the parties to coordinate an in-person hand-off at Luigi's or the Waffle House on the Bobby Jones Expressway; simply place the prized thing in an envelope and leave it with Clyde. Of course, both trading partners tipped the middleman. Ten bucks here, twenty bucks there... Clyde once rented an idle badge for a few hours to a desperate would-be patron for $25. He eventually started buying and selling, but only with people he knew. As a result, Badges Plus Inc. was formed.

"I'd been inside a septic tank for a twenty-five percent commission on a fifty-dollar sale," Pilcher laughed. "But this shit was profitable!" I got so busy that it was difficult to find parking."

Clyde's eyes light up as he tells amazing stories from a life well lived, from glory days at Tubman Junior High to the Big Fight at Richmond Academy, a titanic ten-minute scuffle with Bill Paine—no relation to the Augusta National chairman of the same name—that ended in a tie; to all the adventure of being the more or less official Sewer Service of the Augusta National clubhouse and its cabins, and how all Budget Sewer services had to be His invitation to play the Big Course on Vendor Day in May was apparently cancelled on the spur of the moment. Then locate another plumber, Clyde said.

"It cost them a fortune to replace us," he explains. "I had to bring someone in from Atlanta." The following year, they dug up more fairways and connected to the city sewer line." There was the day a

friend of his drove up with so much badge-related cash in his trunk—
$150,000—that the poor fellow shook like a leaf on a tree and instantly and permanently withdrew from the badge business. Don't say it can't happen, but the astute Budget Sewer man devised a strategy in case someone in his badge system died.

Pilcher, almost unintentionally, became a flipper, purchasing and selling more plots of real estate surrounding the National, and he earned handsomely on that as well. "Paid $280,000 for those two lots," the impoverished boy who got rich claims. "Sold them for three million dollars..."

Back to badges: What does the ranking expert predict for the 2020 Masters market?

"What about next year?" A lot is riding on Tiger. If he's playing well, I think they'll start at $8,000. $10,000 is possible."

A badge's face value in 2019 was, interestingly, $375.

Woods, Couples, and Thomas left the area after their shots were skipped off the pond water and their practice rounds were completed. It started to rain. There was thunder and lightning. Customers were asked to leave.

Tuesday, April 9

Tuesday's customers were not enticed to sleep in despite the comforting pitter patter of rain on the roof. Instead, the $750 practice round viewers arrived in the joyful April gloom like a waterproof army before sun-up, their car headlights flashing off the black, rain-slick streets. They donned ponchos or opened umbrellas, passed through the Masters' TSA-style check-in, and then scarfed down a biscuit or purchased shirts and hats. There wasn't a lot of golf to watch. Play was called off at ten a.m. due to a downpour and the prospect of thunderstorms.

Woods would consider not playing on this day to be one of his best decisions all week. Instead, he stayed on the practice field and did his drills, conserving energy. "On Tuesday, when it just hosed down rain, the course got opened up," he told Henni Zuel, "and all the guys who went out and played said it was useless to be out there because it was gonna be so much faster on Thursday."

With no practice round to contend with, father Tiger had more time to spend with his pups. He was pleased to have Sam and Charlie with him because they had been in Scotland the previous summer, he said. "They were there for me when I failed," he explained. "The last time they came out, I was in contention for the Open Championship." They could feel Dad on top of the board... and I lost. That was terrible."

Failed, was defeated, and sucked. This remark revealed or reminded us of something significant about Tiger. Perhaps the easiest way to comprehend him is as the special ops military man he aspired to be like his father. Missions were defined, and they were either completed or not. When the mission is winning and you finish tied for sixth, you have failed. Others might be able to find something positive in a top ten finish in a major, but not this semi-SEAL.

With two holes to go, Woods had a chance against the infuriatingly consistent Francesco Molinari, 35, a Euro Tour player who never appeared to make a bogey and with whom Tiger was partnered. As you may recall, Carnoustie looked like nuclear winter that week, with its tan, drought-stricken fairways rolling as quickly as Augusta National's sloping greens. However, holes against the wind were difficult as usual, so Molinari, who was then tied for the lead with Xander Schauffele, had to rely on his two-iron second shot to the terrible seventeenth, the penultimate hole. And he got it right. Tiger's second wasn't as good, nor was his birdie try, which continued the day's pattern. He was two points behind.

On this day, eighteen—Jean van de Velde's Waterloo in the infamous Open of 1999—was merely a drive and a flip. Francesco struck a better drive than Tiger (despite the fact that some moron yelled during Tiger's backswing), a little better second, and he made his putt from six feet after Tiger missed his from seven. An Italian man was named Champion Golfer of the Year for the first time.

Molinari!

Given that result, as well as what happened two months later in France, Tiger could be forgiven for making the name of his new opponent a curse. Just as Jerry Seinfeld's TV character despised Wayne Knight's character—Newman!—the charming, well-liked singer from Turin must have crept inside Tiger's skin.

After all of the flag-raising, anthem-playing, and toasting to brotherhood and sportsmanship, the knives finally came out on September 28 at the Albatros course at Le Golf National in suburban Paris for the first Ryder Cup matches. Team USA won the first three matches, winning, winning, and winning. The fourth match pitted the two most ferocious opponents on the American side—Woods and Reed—against the new Open champion and his partner, the long-haired Englishman, Tommy Fleetwood. Patrick and Tiger moved two holes up, giving the red, white, and blue a four-hole advantage, but Frankie and Tommy came back to win the game 3 & 1. Team Europe won all four afternoon matches for the first time in Ryder Cup history, with Molinari and Fleetwood defeating Justin Thomas and Jordan Spieth 5 and 4.

The next morning, Furyk replaced Reed/Woods in the third match. And, by the way, their opponents would be Molinari/Fleetwood once more. The same vexing outcome occurred. Furyk selected a desperate option after lunch: he would play his creaking, forty-two-year-old stud a second time, and let's pray his vertebrae don't come unbolted. Captain Jim paired Tiger with Ryder Cup rookie Bryson DeChambeau, who is twenty-five years old.

You can guess who the opponents were and who won if you don't already know.

Molinari!

On Sunday, Fleetwood was beaten in the singles by Tony Finau, but his fourball and foursomes partner triumphed again, becoming the first European player to achieve the maximum five points. Francesco had Molinaried Tiger's ass four times in two months, including the Open.

He was a difficult man to despise, regardless of which flag you flew. He had a sense of humour: Francesco and Tommy made a 52-second film of them laying in bed with the Ryder Cup between them the morning after... whatever. How did it go for you? Francesco inquires. Tommy responds, "I'd give you a five out of five, Frankie."

During the Tuesday practice session, every member of both Ryder Cup teams worked. The course's high traffic parts were degraded by Woodstock-level mud. Squeegee squads worked around the clock. As if they were defusing bombs, practice tee instructors scrutinised their students' swings. However, some of the males had to cut their efforts short. Woods, Reed, Spieth, Phil Mickelson, Bubba Watson, and Sergio Garcia all had dinner reservations.

They returned to the club freshly showered and nearly similarly dressed, having confronted the annual question: what colour tie best matches a green jacket? Mickelson ('06, '10) goes with red tonight, whereas Nicklaus ('63, '65, '66, '72, '75, '86) always goes with yellow. Again with the adverb.

The Champions Dinner is like a time capsule or a funeral rehearsal, but with more laughs and champagne. Craig Stadler ('82) has taken on the appearance of Wilford Brimley. José-Mara Olazábal ('94, '99) exudes the aura of the Most Interesting Man in the World. Tiger Woods ('97, '01, '02, '05) reminds us that male pattern baldness runs in families and that time flies without a Nike Aerobill Classic 99 hat on his head.

Ben Hogan founded the Dinner in 1952 in gratitude for his win in 1951, following close misses in 1942 (a playoff defeat to Byron Nelson) and 1946 (a three-putt on the final green that turned Herm Keiser's long arms into a green jacket). Initially, just the defending champ picked up the tab for the previous champs, but at some point, the defender began to choose the bill of fare as well—though going off-menu has never been an issue. In 1989, Sandy Lyle ('88), a Scot, served haggis as a starter. "I didn't eat that," Charles Coody ('71) recalls. "I knew exactly what it was."

The club issues the participants with two clubhouse badges and an honorarium substantial enough for Coody to at least seem to be interested in cooked sheep intestines combined with onions and oatmeal.

The meal piques everyone's interest. In 1998, Tiger demonstrated that he was still a kid by featuring cheeseburgers and milkshakes. In 2019, Reed demanded more subtle flavours. "I'm definitely going to fatten everyone up," he declared, then demonstrated how. The bone-in ribeye with herb butter would be the main course. Mac & cheese, creamed spinach, and corn crème brûlée were served as sides. The wines were Napa Valley Chardonnay and Cabernet Sauvignon. Chocolate crunch and praline cheesecake were among the dessert selections.

Mountain trout was the healthy entrée choice for 1971 champ Charles Coody, and it was delicious. The entire evening was enjoyable. However, it was not a particularly enjoyable or interesting interlude because the present lineup lacks a storyteller to spin a postprandial yarn or two. Claude Harmon, Jimmy Demaret, Gene Sarazen, Henry Picard, and, most notably, Sam Snead could be relied on for amusing or revealing anecdotes and dirty jokes—read: Snead—but they are all no longer with us. Jack Burke, Jr. enjoys declaiming and can be a spellbinder, but he is now 96 years old and hasn't returned to Augusta in several years.

Tiger, how about you?

"Tiger doesn't talk much," Coody observed. "However, he appears to have turned over a new leaf." He appears to be more approachable. I believe he has matured much."

Some of the oldsters became tired of the dinner after a while. Perhaps everything does. "It used to be fun," Sarazen ('34) told me in 1997, at the age of 95. "But the room is now too small." There are too many of them (other previous Masters champions), and they all want hats and other items signed so they can sell them at their clubs."

"What happens is you get to the point where you don't even know the players," Burke told Murray of The Guardian a few years back. I'm not going back. It's too difficult. For one dinner, you must go 150 miles (from Atlanta). "I don't see the point anymore."

Despite this, it is the one meal that every player craves.

Wednesday, April 10

Gilbert A. Freeman, Director of Golf at Lakewood Country Club in Dallas, is a die-hard Masters fan. He'd rather give up brisket enchiladas than miss April in Augusta, which isn't going to happen. He feels the same way about Eldrick T. Woods: he admires his flair, appearance, temperament, and accomplishment. And Gilbert backs up his words by stocking the Lakewood golf shop with plenty of Nike.

"I sat behind him on the range on Wednesday and watched him hit balls, just like I always do," Freeman says. "He was tearing it. A light show with lasers. Never missed a single shot. Later, I was on the phone with my team. 'I'm betting on Tiger,' I said.

"He appears to be instructor-free at the moment." Matt Killen appears to be little more than an extra set of eyes."

Tiger paused his swing, established eye contact with his companions, and the four of them strolled from the practice range behind the clubhouse to the tenth tee. "I followed him out onto the course for his nine-hole practice round with Couples, Kevin Kisner, and Justin Thomas," says Freeman. "And he was grinning and jacking around while still killing the ball." He was the least uptight I'd ever seen."

These four had to finish by one o'clock, since the Big Course, as members call it, would close for final primping, as it always does, while the focus shifted to the Little Course. No one calls it that; it's the Par 3 Golf Course, and it's the living legacy of club and tournament co-founder Cliff Roberts, despite the fact that Cliff shot and killed himself by the banks of one of the course's two ponds on a dark night seventeen years ago.

From the competition's inception in 1934 through 1959, the club hosted a variety of festivities on the day or days preceding the tournament. Long driving contests were common, and a large elderly boy named George Bayer was generally the winner. They did have a bow and arrow show at one point. The first Masters Festival procession, in 1957, went down Broad Street downtown, with marching bands, floats, and golf pros waving to the fans—are they still patrons when they're not on campus?—According to the Chronicle, there were 25,000 of them that first year, with the golf heroes riding in white Oldsmobile and Cadillac convertibles. Contestants in the Miss Golf Pageant competed in gown, swimsuit, talent, and three-putt avoidance. We're joking about the three-putt, but the club had a strong desire to attract and retain fans back when golf alone wasn't enough to assure the tournament's future.

The benign dictator of Augusta National wanted to try something new as well. In a letter to the membership in 1958, Roberts recommended constructing a par three course for $67,500. Subscription forms are provided. Despite the fact that he was not an architect, Roberts rode herd on the thing so hard that he merits co-designer credit with George Cobb. It was a tremendous success. The Par 3 was a favourite from the start, giving a fun, fast way for members and their visitors to warm up for or cool down following a round on the Big Course. On Wednesday of Masters Week, the Par 3 would provide light-hearted competition for former champions and current challengers on holes that currently range from 77 to 151 yards. The Par 3 is a piece of golf nirvana, with images of pink and white flowering dogwoods and colourfully dressed spectators bouncing off the surface of its two reflecting ponds. Because there is no room, viewers do not move; they simply select a position and sit.

"It used to be fun, and then they stopped selling beer," musee Tim Wright, a local raconteur. "Now you have to walk all the way over to the concession stand near the main entrance, get two beers, and they're gone by the time you get back to Par 3." I suppose they want a family vibe. They are welcome to it."

It's family. Wives, girlfriends, children, and Patton Kizzire's mother all looked adorable in white caddy jumpsuits and green headgear. A footnote: Matt Wallace, an English pro from suburban London, won in a playoff with Sandy Lyle. For the second year in a row, a towering Polynesian Mormon stole the Par 3 spotlight from the cute kids and polite legends.

As you may recall, in April of 2018, Masters rookie Milton Pouha "Tony" Finau arrived at the eighth tee with the largest entourage of any participant. His attractive wife Alayna and the couple's four young children surrounded him as he chose a gap wedge for the 121-yard shot. When dad spun his shot into the hole, Team Finau leaped and cheered along with everyone else. Tony as well. He threw his club in the air, rushed forward twenty or thirty yards in ecstasy—a excellent high school hoopster, he is fairly light on his feet—pirouetted to gaze at Alayna and the youngsters, and suddenly, in the midst of this wild celebration: Finau falls!

The video was infected with germs. It's gone viral.

Finau repositioned his ankle almost as quickly as he dislocated it. Alayna raced to her husband's side. "Oh my gosh, dude," she exclaimed. "Did you really just pop your ankle back into place?" He had, and it hurt like hell, but he limped through the final Par 3 hole before asking his agent to get an orthopedist, a magnetic resonance imaging machine, and aspirin. Of course, it would be a shame for anyone to miss the Masters due to such a peculiar (but humorous) mishap. But, if Finau where to send his regrets in the morning, he'd undoubtedly think of Tiger and April 1997.

Tony, aged seven, sat riveted by the TV on the couch in the Finals' packed Salt Lake City home that frigid weekend. He'd never seen a golf event before this. "I saw this kid who was the same colour as me," he remembered. "I watched Tiger Woods win the Masters at the exact moment I began." "I looked at it and I'm like, man, maybe I can do that someday, maybe I can play in the Masters... [but] I didn't dream of just playing in the Masters, I dreamed of winning it."

"It's impossible to overestimate Tiger's influence on kids like me, or the impact he's had on golf in general."

Tony's father, Kelepi, was from the Kingdom of Tonga, a remote Pacific island nation that leads the globe in corruption and obesity. He immigrated to the United States with his family when he was eleven years old. He met and married Ravena, a Polynesian, and managed to keep his family afloat on $35,000 a year. Delta and Western Airlines both paid him to handle their bags. While Kelepi Finau didn't know much about golf, he was a great athlete who understood how sports might keep kids too occupied for trouble. Outside the doors, there was turmoil in the form of easy access to drugs and gangs in their underprivileged area. Many Pacific Islanders had gathered in Salt Lake City, as did the Tongan Crip Gang, the Sons of Samoa, and other similar juvenile organisations from Los Angeles. The Finau brothers would not be attending.

Kelepi scrounge for Salvation Army equipment and golf balls. He borrowed Golf My Way from the library and laboriously devoured Jack Nicklaus' instructional expertise. He also laid carpet strips on the garage floor and hung an old mattress from the ceiling beams. Tony fired from one side of the rug, while his younger brother fired from the other, aiming at spray-painted targets marked low, middle, and high. When the weather in Utah warmed up, Gipper and Tony Finau wore out the practice green at a neighbouring par three course. They did not participate since they could not afford the green charge.

"We hit tens of thousands of chips, maybe millions," Tony stated. "At Jordan River's par 3 course, we learned what it's like to make the right sound when making a solid chip."

A watershed moment happened, thankfully not uncommon in golf: the pro, Richard Mason, recognized the twins' talent and desire and began to let them play for free. Tony noticed the severity of Jordan River mosquitos on the course, which encouraged him to wear high socks and play fast, habits he carried into adulthood. Many years later, he was on the verge of achieving his childhood desire, one foot swelling and turning purple. He played anyway—with a limp—and established his fame, finishing tied for tenth with 68-74-73-66, well behind the victor, Reed, but good enough for an invitation to return. Given his failure the previous year, no one could blame Finau for skipping the Par 3s in 2019. Instead, he and his agency, Wasserman, and his equipment company, Nike, created a mockumentary about the invention of the Nike Finaul, footwear designed to avoid ankle injuries during celebrations. The video was published immediately before the Masters. It's pretty nice; the star delivers a lot of deadpan banter. "I'm most proud of having a shoe that can help others," Tony explains. "And when they get a hole-in-one and want to celebrate, they know which shoe to put on."

The joke was understood by all. On every hole, Tony's large ugly green Finau golf boot drew a laugh.

Thursday, April 11

9:58 Finau, Sergio Garcia, Henrik Stenson

11:04 Woods, Jon Rahm, Haotong Li

1:16 Molinari, Rafa Cabrera-Bello, Tyrrell Hatton

2:00 Koepka, Jordan Spieth, Paul Casey

The Honorary Starters emerged in the early morning light, hours before Tony, Tiger, Frankie, and Brooks gulped in cleansing breaths and took aim at the green, green grass to the left of the blindingly white granulated quartz fairway bunker.

After a lengthy introduction, Augusta National Chairman Fred Ridley remarked, "Ladies and gentlemen, from South Africa, Gary Player." The little man in black, who was eighty-three years old, looked fantastic. He's been a fitness fanatic and public figure his entire life. "Feel that stomach!" he exclaimed to many astonished strangers. "Like iron!" says one. And, from what I've observed, individuals occasionally gave him the poke he desired, although uncomfortably.

A player whacked a ball along the fairway with a swing that was a close match to the one that won the Masters three times.

Years have not been kind to the GOAT. Jack Nicklaus, 79, the best golfer of all time in terms of majors won (eighteen) and Masters won (six), is drooping and slumping as a result of excess weight and osteoarthritis. The 2019 Masters had begun when the Golden Bear in a yellow sweater whacked one up the middle well short of Gary's ball, waved dismissively at his effort, and the 2019 Masters had begun.

That was only the phrase for what was about to happen on the first hole's tee and every other par four and par five, because to see Finau and Koepka whack a driver was to watch a suborbital voyage into the stratosphere. The fact that the ball travels far further than it used to is undeniable, but what to do about it is. Members of Augusta National have been particularly irritated and discommoded by golf's inability to curb its distance fetish, as they own one-fourth of the majors and roughly half of the traditions. All other sports have an official ball, but it's excellent business for golf ball manufacturers to have sliced and diced the pill into many permutations of spin and flight, as well as compounds, construction, and colour, and we're now convinced we need them all.

What about a dead Masters ball? This could link the tournament to its past. Chairman Ridley, the 1975 US Amateur champion and current USGA president, blasted down the proposal in his yearly (since 2017) press conference. According to reports, the club will continue to extend its length and grow trees. For example, the forty yards added to the fifth hole in 2019 made an already difficult hole even more difficult. The landing area for drives on this 495-yard par four is now a difficult upslope, and the green is insane.

With the recent purchase of acreage from its Rae's Creek neighbour, Augusta Country Club, Augusta National may even lengthen its thirteenth hole, one of the best and most famous courses in golf yet the easiest hole in the Masters.

"Is your course long enough yet?" I enquired of an insider.

"I don't know," he or she said. "Right now, we're waiting to see if the USGA, R&A, or PGA Tour will do anything about the ball."

Lee Trevino simplified it all for me a few years ago: The trampoline effect, spin rates, cubic centimetres in driver heads, and golf giving the thumbs down to the curve-it-left, bend-it-right shot creator game he played were all discussed. Trevino blamed the USGA, not Augusta National.

"They complain that the Masters lengthens the course." But do you believe the public wants Tiger Woods to hit a three-iron off every tee? That customer isn't going to pay [a small fortune] to see that. He desires the homerun ball.

"What they should do is increase the diameter of the ball to 1.72 and take an eighth of an ounce off."

They might have had that conversation if Nicklaus and Woods had sat together at the Dinner the night before. For many years, Jack has been vociferous about reeling in the ball. Tiger Woods won the Open at St. Andrews' Old Course in 2005, flying his tee balls over bunkers that had ensnared golfers for decades. More proof that something isn't right, Jack added; he was by far the strongest man in golf when he won the Open at St. Andrews in 1970 and 1978, but those sand pits were in play for him.

The Honorary Starters emerged in the early morning light, hours before Tony, Tiger, Frankie, and Brooks gulped in cleansing breaths and took aim at the green, green grass to the left of the blindingly white granulated quartz fairway bunker.

After a lengthy introduction, Augusta National Chairman Fred Ridley remarked, "Ladies and gentlemen, from South Africa, Gary Player." The little man in black, who was eighty-three years old, looked fantastic. He's been a fitness fanatic and public figure his entire life. "Feel that stomach!" he exclaimed to many astonished strangers. "Like iron!" says one. And, from what I've observed, individuals occasionally gave him the poke he desired, although uncomfortably.

A player whacked a ball along the fairway with a swing that was a close match to the one that won the Masters three times.

Years have not been kind to the GOAT. Jack Nicklaus, 79, the best golfer of all time in terms of majors won (eighteen) and Masters won (six), is drooping and slumping as a result of excess weight and osteoarthritis. The 2019 Masters had begun when the Golden Bear in a yellow sweater whacked one up the middle well short of Gary's ball, waved dismissively at his effort, and the 2019 Masters had begun.

That was only the phrase for what was about to happen on the first hole's tee and every other par four and par five, because to see Finau and Koepka whack a driver was to watch a suborbital voyage into the stratosphere. The fact that the ball travels far further than it used to is undeniable, but what to do about it is. Members of Augusta National have been particularly irritated and discommoded by golf's inability to curb its distance fetish, as they own one-fourth of the majors and roughly half of the traditions. All other sports have an official ball, but it's excellent business for golf ball manufacturers to have sliced and diced the pill into many permutations of spin and flight, as well as compounds, construction, and colour, and we're now convinced we need them all.

What about a dead Masters ball? This could link the tournament to its past. Chairman Ridley, the 1975 US Amateur champion and current USGA president, blasted down the proposal in his yearly (since 2017) press conference. According to reports, the club will continue to extend its length and grow trees. For example, the forty yards added to the fifth hole in 2019 made an already difficult hole even more difficult. The landing area for drives on this 495-yard par four is now a difficult upslope, and the green is insane.

With the recent purchase of acreage from its Rae's Creek neighbour, Augusta Country Club, Augusta National may even lengthen its thirteenth hole, one of the best and most famous courses in golf yet the easiest hole in the Masters.

"Is your course long enough yet?" I enquired of an insider.

"I don't know," he or she said. "Right now, we're waiting to see if the USGA, R&A, or PGA Tour will do anything about the ball."

Lee Trevino simplified it all for me a few years ago: The trampoline effect, spin rates, cubic centimetres in driver heads, and golf giving the thumbs down to the curve-it-left, bend-it-right shot creator game he played were all discussed. Trevino blamed the USGA, not Augusta National.

"They complain that the Masters lengthens the course." But do you believe the public wants Tiger Woods to hit a three-iron off every tee? That customer isn't going to pay [a small fortune] to see that. He desires the homerun ball.

"What they should do is increase the diameter of the ball to 1.72 and take an eighth of an ounce off."

They might have had that conversation if Nicklaus and Woods had sat together at the Dinner the night before. For many years, Jack has been vociferous about reeling in the ball. Tiger Woods won the Open at St. Andrews' Old Course in 2005, flying his tee balls over bunkers that had ensnared golfers for decades. More proof that something isn't right, Jack added; he was by far the strongest man in golf when he won the Open at St. Andrews in 1970 and 1978, but those sand pits were in play for him.

This Masters Week, the stories on most pens and in most media lips had been the potential of Tiger, of course, and Brooks Koepka's body, because there was a lot less of it and people wanted to know why on earth there was less. Brooks stated he'd lost roughly twenty-five pounds, but he wouldn't say why. When he was chastised for it during his post-round press conference, he reacted with haiku-like simplicity: "I lift too many weights and I'm too big to play golf."And then I'm too small when I lose weight.

"I'll make myself happy." "I'm doing it for myself, and obviously it appears to work," I don't care what anyone else says.

He'd just shot 66 and was tied for the lead after the opening round of the Masters. The nerveless, brilliant athlete birdied five out of six, beginning with the dead-easy twelfth, which required only a three-quarter nine iron and a putt from the edge. It was an exciting time to be Brooks. The geometrical, symmetrical former Florida State Seminole had risen to world number one and was still climbing, having finished first, first, and second in the previous three US Opens, and first and first in the previous two PGA Championships. What a resume he now had, and what a life he was leading. I'd ask him about becoming the 2004 Sir Henry Cotton Rookie of the Year on the European Tour if we were having cocktails. And probably about his fit and attractive girlfriend, Ms. Jena Sims, who appeared in Sharknado 5: Global Swarming.

Tiger posted a two-under-par 70 and was pleased with his performance. "I've shot this number and won four coats before, so hopefully I can do it again," he explained. In reality, only three of his four victories had begun with a seven oh. He'd dialled the erroneous number in the first round in 2005, but then set the world right by finishing with sixty-six, sixty-five, and seventy-one, forcing a playoff with Chris DiMarco, which Tiger won. That was his last victory in Augusta, fourteen years earlier, but it seemed much further away.

Molinari birdied fifteen and eighteen to tie Woods for the lead with seventy.

Finau finished with a 71. He didn't put on the boots.

As night fell, everyone in town had a great time. Clouds and cooler air moved in from the north and west.

Friday, April 12

Don M. Wilson III shifted into drive, his 2004 BMW 330ci in the rearview mirror. With his hands at ten and two and the radio turned to Motown and BBC podcasts of "In Our Time," he sped south from

Connecticut past New York City, Jersey, and Philadelphia on I-95, the longest north-south road in the United States and the fourth-busiest interstate. The MapQuest directions were straightforward: take I-95 south for 777 miles. Take the Bull Street exit. And then you're there, "there" being the Comfort Inn in Columbia, South Carolina for the exhausted retired banker. Winter was still gripping the country when Wilson left early that Tuesday morning, but in the Palmetto State's capital, mild air and spots and blots of pink, scarlet, and white bloomers proclaimed the arrival of spring. The journey had lasted eleven and a half hours.

Wilson met his son, Rob, an Indiana University graduate who is now pursuing another degree at the Johns Hopkins University School of Advanced International Studies, who flew in from D.C. the next morning. The Columbia airport is located on the west side of town, and Augusta is only a one-hour drive away. The Wilsons had Par 3 tickets.

"Wonderful," Wilson commented later. "What a brilliant idea. You're up close and personal with the players. It's really casual, with no competing vibe."

Wilson had never been to the Masters before, which seemed strange because it is rare to find a more enthusiastic and hooked-up golfer, or one who is less tolerant of meandering during a round. DMW3, as his pals refer to him, can race walk to an eight. He's an Anglophile who's seen "at least twenty" Open Championships. Wilson demonstrates his enthusiasm for the game by authoring strange and fascinating books about it, in addition to membership at such gemlike courses as The SandHills in Nebraska and Garden City in New York. Machrihanish: Machaire Shanais Golf 1880s-1920s is the ninth and most recent slip-cased, limited edition product from Grant Books—H.R.J. Grant of Droitwich, Worcestershire, England is Wilson's publishing partner. Machrihanish is a heartbreakingly beautiful links course in a rural part of Scotland; machaire shanais is Scottish Gaelic meaning "plain of whispers." Grant & Wilson's

Edwardian Golf Library 1900-1914 is still accessible to Chapter Six, "Poetry and Songs."

The Wilsons, like every other Augusta National first-timer, were astounded by what they witnessed on Thursday and Friday.

"It's one of the greatest outdoor spaces in the world," DMW3 stated. "It's a horticultural treasure that also happens to feature an extremely nice golf course... In comparison to an Open, there are fewer spectator stands and considerably fewer people. I liked the no-cellphones regulation, as well as the non-digitized scoreboards and their scarcity. At an Open, they have live radio, but not at Augusta. But it's fun not knowing the score every now and again... It's overstaffed, which is fantastic. The personnel make you feel like you're a guest of a family, not a corporation."

Koepka birdied the first hole, then shot a big fat hook off two into a thickly treed area known as "the Delta ticket counter" by golfer/comedians of yore—the apparent joke being that being left on two leads to an early flight out of Augusta, Columbia, or Atlanta. Brooks double-bogeyed the seventh hole and was two over for the day after six holes, but he rebounded and finished with a 71 in a tie for first place.

"There's no point in getting too excited on a Friday," Koepka said later. "You've still got a lot of golf to play, so you've just got to hang in there."

Molinari and a few others took the lead. His 67, which included a deuce on the easy twelfth, was made up of thirteen pars and five birdies. His consistent performance at the Open, the most recent Ryder Cup, and this week in Augusta gave him an aura of unflappability that flipped the national cliché on its head. He wasn't the tenor in the opera, but rather the ticket taker in the lobby. Not a hot-blooded and temperamental Latino, but a quiet and self-contained strategist—perhaps a Russian chess champion?

Molinari didn't have the personality for it, but as previously stated, he and Tiger had a friendly rivalry.As they say in Hollywood, they'd met cute. Francesco and his brother Edoardo had agreed that whomever qualified for the Masters first would get the other brother as a caddy. Edoardo won the 2005 US Amateur, earning him an entry to Augusta and a first-round partnering with the defending champion—Tiger—and a sherpa he'd known his entire life.

"After a few holes, both Tiger and Steve Williams approached my brother and said, 'There's a man playing on the European tour [who's] doing well with a name similar to yours,' and my brother says, 'Yeah, he's my brother.'

"'Does he play this week? "What is he doing?"'No, no, he's over there,' says my brother. 'In white overalls.'"

It had not been a pleasant experience for Francesco. "I didn't really enjoy caddying," he admitted. "Standing with the bag, waiting for him to hit the shots seemed like a nightmare." Caddieing isn't much fun around here."

The hills and those terrible oven-like coveralls, unspoken by the courteous Molinari, are two other things that make carrying a suitcase in the Masters a beat-down. It's time for a miracle fabric or an entirely other look—maybe culottes.

Molinari's game proceeded slowly but steadily. He earned his first invitations to the Masters, where he placed 30th, and to Europe's Ryder Cup team in 2010. In the Sunday singles, he faced Tiger. The American triumphed, but America was defeated. Francesco's sang froid—in Italian, a sangue freddo—earned him the most nerve-racking spot in the batting order, the final match on the final day, at the next Cup, the 2012 edition at Medinah Country Club in suburban Chicago. He'd have another game against Tiger.

In what was either the most spectacular breakdown or the most thrilling comeback in Ryder Cup history, Team Europe rallied from a four-point deficit to win the Match. Woods and Molinari each tied. Nobody mentioned a burgeoning rivalry.

Back at the Masters, no one except Finau's friends and family noticed him shooting 71 on Friday. But be patient. On Saturday, he would set fire to the globe.

Tiger teed off at 2:18, half an hour later than planned. The pokiness of the field was caused by the rain. He'd been awake for some time; his day had begun while it was still dark as night. Tiger had hoisted his Titleist Scotty Cameron Newport while the others in his opulent rented property at The River Golf Club were undoubtedly sleeping. 2 putters from his Monster Energy golf bag indicated "walk time" to the dog, and man and beast slipped out the door.

The pawprints and footprints in the dew indicated that they travelled across a road-side fairway and then to a green, where Tiger did what he does best: he rolled some putts. In the dead of night, a couple of maintenance workers drove up to inspect the mysterious golfer. "He couldn't have been nicer," recalls Chris Verdery, Director of Golf at the club. "They simply discussed his late start time that day and took a few selfies." I appreciate how he just pretended to be an ordinary guy. He was definitely not practising because we had Bermuda greens and Augusta National had bentgrass."

And yet: Tiger would roll in, let's see... 132 feet of birdie putts this day, including increments of 25, 30, and 37. Back in his peak, the made long putt was a mainstay of his game; had those glory days returned? On practically every green, he received standing ovations simply for being Tiger. It was the closest he'd gone to the halfway lead at the Masters in fourteen years when he concluded his round with a 68 that put him within a shot of the lead. The magnetic man's popularity grew even stronger now that he had a chance to win.

He was known as the People's Champion. Despite Molinari, DJ, Koepka, Rose, Rory, and Spieth; despite the back, past, and passage of time; despite everything, Tiger was the king until further notice.

How did he appear? We questioned a witness.

"Utterly composed," DMW3 responded.

Saturday, April 13

Donna Archer arrived early, like she always did, and walked Augusta National backwards, from 18 to 1, as she always did. She'd said hello to the usual suspects, dear old pals she'd only seen once a year lately: Tom Watson, Gary Player, the Langers, the Coodys, the Norths, the Azingers, and Jack and Barb Nicklaus. Mrs. Archer is a vibrant, cheery woman, but this year she felt the heavy weight of nostalgia more than usual, because this tournament marked the fiftieth anniversary of her late husband's improbable victory in the 1969 Masters over numerous more well-known rivals, namely Tom Weiskopf and Billy Casper. By the way, Tom would go on to be a four-time Masters runner-up; Billy would win the tournament the following year.

Mrs. Archer came to the twelfth hole and took a breather.

"George always played twelve very cautiously." "It wasn't a particularly noticeable hole for him," Donna said. "But he was paired with Weiskopf—or was in the group right behind him—when Tom put a hundred balls in the water."

It was not one hundred. However, a full-immersion baptism of five balls in Rae's Creek plus a couple of putts tallied up to a double-quintuple, or ten-over 13. Corner, amen, and let us pray. We've joked that twelve is simple, but everyone knows that it's not, partially because the air above it swirls like a banana in a blender. And it's not just the wind that makes this 155-yard throw to a patch of green ice one of the most difficult holes on the course. It has been significantly more difficult to par than TPC Sawgrass' famous island green sixteenth.

The stories you hear... picture the following two victims telling their stories while shining a flashlight under their chins on a dark, dark night:

"It was a Friday, and I was playing pretty well, and I looked fine with the cut," D.A. Weibring explained. "And then I got to twelve." The pin was back because of the wind. I hit a six iron that landed six feet from the pin, then slid into the back bunker. Now I have the most difficult shot in the world, a downhill lie, a downhill shot, no green, and Rae's Creek awaiting me. To cut a long tale short, I built a six-footer for an eight."

Except for the crackle and pop of the campfire, the night is silent. Weibring, triumphant, passes the torch to Bob Gilder.

"The first year my son ever caddied for me, I was one shot off the lead on the second day." The light quickly reflects off the gleam in Gilder's eyes. "I kept hitting good shots on the back nine that just didn't work out." A bogey on eleven, followed by a seven or eight on the par three..."

Even the greatest among us have had to endure mocking from the twelfth hole, just as rain falls equally on the fair and the unjust. Jordan Spieth bogied ten and eleven with five shots in hand and only nine to play in 2016, but he hammered his nine iron at the back right flag on twelve and didn't make it. Then he dropped a ball, tried again, and failed. The resulting quadruple bogey seven gave Danny Noonan—no, sorry, Danny Willett—an improbable victory. As of this writing, he is the sole player on the PGA Tour.

The crusty old green-jacketed co-founders rolled down the hill in a cart one year in the 1960s to see Jones favourite Jack Nicklaus play number twelve, which was a huge event because Bobby was terminally ill with a neurological condition and was getting out of his cabin less and less each year. Jack noticed Jones and Roberts parked to the side. The vast throng fell silent. Jack performed the stations of his elaborate pre-shot ritual. Finally, the deliberate golfer swung— and whistled a shank over Cliff and Bobby's heads.

Donna Archer finished her backward tour of the cathedral in the woods and remembered her late husband. On another bright April day fifty years ago, George Archer, the tallest-ever major winner and one of the game's best putters, shrugged his way to a 42L and the crowd erupted.

She'd passed our dramatis personae on her lengthy walk when they were filming sixty-four (Finau), sixty-six (Molinari), a sixty-seven for Tiger, and a sixty-nine for Koepka. Amazing work! It's now time for some italics.

Tony Finau almost eagled three holes on the front nine, lipped out a bunker shot on two, a pitch on three, and then created history on eight, the uphill, left-bending, hardest par five on the course. Almost. Bruce Devlin spotted a favourable lie for his Dot just in the right rough on this same hole fifty-two Masters before. The Australian had 248 yards to the unnoticed flagstick. He hit a hook with a wooden four wood and dared if the ball didn't roll in.

It was 1967. In 2019, Finau had 230 yards to the front edge and 261 yards to the pole on what is now a considerably longer hole—"a comfortable four iron for me," he stated. As they say, he poured it, and his ball almost did a Devlin, halting a baby's foot away. He had a ten-footer on nine for a twenty-nine after the tap-in eagle, which would have been the lowest-ever first-half score in Masters history— but his Bettinardi Precision Milled Putter was a bit off this time.

When he met with the press a few hours later, the conversation was of the unusually early start planned for Sunday due to impending poor weather late in the afternoon, and the prospect of him being matched with Tiger.

"It would be an unbelievable thing for me... a dream come true for me," Tony added, although he didn't appear as impressed as his words suggested. "Tiger taught us how to compete," on the other hand. You should not be afraid of anyone. He's up against players he's bred."

Finau was easily the best of The Four at the media give-and-take for around eighteen minutes, a credit to the askers; his desire to understand, his disarming style, and a frequent smile made him easily the finest of The Four.

"Being Tongan and Samoan is a huge part of who I am," he said to a question rarely asked in polite company. "We're a driven bunch. We're also really laid back. "I enjoy having a good time on the golf course."

Molinari saved a par on the eighteenth with a superb long bunker shot, making it his forty-third consecutive hole without a bogey. The "clean card" meant a lot to him; during his brief interrogation, he was more proud of his par putts on four and five than of the six birdies he'd scored.

Francesco, you have a two-shot advantage. What do you have planned for tomorrow?

Plan! Molinari smirked at the thought. "A few guys are going to try to derail my plan," he said. He was monotonous in his second language, and he appeared tired—after all the hillwalking, focus, and stress, why wouldn't he be? "I just need to do my job and do it well and see if that's good enough."

Tiger in purple had given the crowd what they wanted: superb golf that resulted with birdies and one or two muffled fist pumps. Following that, he answered journalists' queries under the gigantic, ancient water oak by the clubhouse—The Tree—rather than the sleek new Press Center. He made a lighthearted remark regarding the next day's early start hour. The press questioned him... something. Something was spoken by Tiger. We've heard this man interviewed so many times, and he's typically so boring that I think we shut out his words and just look for emotion on that extraordinary face, and listen to his diction: short phrases punctuated by extended breaks and rising inflection—uptalking. Comedian Conor Moore has his Tiger sniff, tug the collar of his red shirt, cough, turn away, and comment that "it's really tough out there."

What Woods did that night in his lovely rental property between the wide brown Savannah River and a golf course is not recorded in history. He may have raised a glass to the great folks at the Texas Back Institute Center for Disc Replacement at some time. Another day, vertebrae!

Koepka spoke at the media centre about his thoughts. He's a breath of new air, a brilliant golfer who seems to appreciate both the art and science of the greatest game. He plays fast, is irritated by those who don't, and has a strict policy against complaining about course conditions or weather. He sounded genuinely perplexed or amused by the nerdy queries, and he continued to sound wise. These slogans might, and perhaps should, be embroidered on golf towels. Here's some more Kafka wisdom. Koepka.

"I've been playing this game for twenty-two or twenty-three years; nothing will change overnight."I understand how to play the game. "All I know is how to hit the ball.""I'm just going to tee it up, look where I want to hit it, and fire at it," I'm going to say.

CHAPTER 4

THE BACK NINE ON SUNDAY

The Waffle House near the Bobby Jones Expressway quickly filled up. Patrons studied their phones, scanned plastic menus, discussed golf, and wondered if somebody had thought to pack a canteen of Bloody Marys. Waitresses asked, "Whatcha have, hon?" and communicated the orders to the cook, who had his back to the room and scraped and chopped a metal spatula on the sizzling grill as if he had eight arms, like Vishnu. Diners could and did order hash browns spread, covered, smothered, chunked, topped, or peppered; Yankee lads ate grits because when in Rome; they drank gallons of coffee; they tipped lavishly; and then they were gone, for the insanely early start of the 2019 Masters. Balls in the air at 7:00 p.m.! It made for an early morning following the previous night.

At 6:59 a.m., no one saw the rising sun, just brightening hues of grey streaming into a cold morning. It would be a lovely day to play or watch, with no need for a jacket. Approximately 72 degrees.

Tiger had gotten up before the grit-munching waffle eaters, putting his feet on the floor at four o'clock. An early morning tee time was a significant annoyance for a guy whose stiff, achy body required a long time to limber up enough to even begin warming up. With terrible weather anticipated for late afternoon, the proactive Augusta National and Masters officials ordered an early start, with play in threesomes rather than pairs, and half the field starting on ten and half on one. Everything was unprecedented.

In the murky grey light, the players carefully rolled their courtesy cars up Magnolia Lane's deep green tunnel. Except for two, they were all dark grey Mercedes-Benz SUVs: Tiger drove a black one and Ricky Fowler drove a green Maybach. Some participants would return in another luxury car in a year, but others might never see this place again.

Patrons coming in from another part of the site were nervous, but also energised by foreboding and promise. Tiger, too, claimed he felt pressure, and that he always did. But it was a routine he was used to and accepted as part of the experience. Recognizing, if not relishing, the high stress of big moments, he didn't have to strive to manage a suddenly jumpy and disorganised brain since, he claimed, his senses intensified as the competition approached its conclusion. He became more concentrated rather than less.

Some argue that the best golf tournament ever played was so spectacular because the three top contenders represented eras as well as themselves. The 1960 US Open at Cherry Hills included Hogan, Palmer, and Nicklaus from the past, present, and future. By the way, the present won. The divisions were less defined in the 2019 Masters. Despite the fact that Koepka and Molinari were clearly significant players in the here and now at the pinnacle of professional golf, and Finau appeared poised to join them in the winner's circle soon, Tiger refused to play the Ghost of Christmas Past. Time, not the other players, is said to be an athlete's worst adversary, but the forty-three-year-old Woods was not giving up. Not yet, at any rate.

They were four genius golfers performing at peak levels. What made them unique? How were they similar?

They were indistinguishable on the surface, since the Cablanasian, Polynesian, Italian, and generic, plain-vanilla Koepka all came on the first tee wearing the same brand of apparel. How humiliating! However, the four at least had a clean appearance because Nike endorsers wear only the swoosh and no competing logos, as opposed to the six, eight, or ten distinct sales messages on the bodies of some other golfers. The simple, uncluttered signage would be worth millions to the major marketer today. When Woods competed in the 2018 Valspar, a regular tour tournament, CNBC business writer

Dominic Chu claimed that Nike received $10.8 million in "brand exposure" from TV and online. The value to the brand was immense with four leading men wearing the swoosh and it being the Masters.

Finau was a mid-major small forward in the game of books and covers; Molinari was a pocket square and a tailored grey suit away from being the CEO of Armani or Ferrari; and Koepka was the all-star left fielder who hits with power to all fields. Given what we know, it's difficult not to imagine Tiger in black clothes, wraparound shades, and a tactical pistol belt in an alternate scenario.

Who is the best athlete? Finau, most likely, because he excelled at basketball's run, leap, catch, and throw, a sport in which he was recruited to play collegiately. He can dunk while standing flat-footed under a hoop. Molinari enjoys skiing and snowboarding. Koepka appears to be a jock. He comes from a baseball family and played as a kid; in Pittsburgh, people still take a knee when Brooks' great uncle, former Pirates shortstop Dick Groat, is mentioned. Except for scuba diving and ping-pong at Ryder Cups, Tiger's only games outside of golf were not sports and required only a sofa and a controller.

Masters records: Tiger Woods' four wins and nine additional top-ten finishes in Augusta dwarfs those of the other three. Koepka's best finish in three tries was a T-11 in 2017 (he didn't play in 2018 due to a wrist injury). Moli's best finish in seven Masters was a T-20; he'd missed the cut twice and wasn't even invited to the party in '15 and '16. Finau, as previously stated, was essentially a blank slate, having only played the competition once before.

Tony is four years old, Tiger is two, Frankie is two, and Brooks is on deck. Tiger has fourteen majors; Brooks has four; Frankie has one; and Tony is on his way. Confidence, technique, momentum, or astrological influence? All three would be quite high on the list.

Koepka is 28 years old, Finau is 29 years old, Molinari is 36 years old, and Woods is 43 years old.

They lived in London, Utah, and Jupiter, Florida, among other places. Molinari was passionate about two soccer clubs: West Ham United in England and Internazionale Milano in Italy. According to his cap, Finau is a Los Angeles Lakers fan. Tiger is frequently spotted courtside at Orlando Magic games.

Molinari, Koepka, and Woods are the only players to have won a major after trailing after three rounds. There was no comparison in terms of fan support. Just as Tinker Bell's clapping hands protected her from dying, fourth-round Masters fans would create a wave of emotion for Tiger to ride. The game began when the fan favourite popped some gum into his mouth.

"Fore, please!" exclaimed the man on the tee. "Tiger Woods, now drivin'."

A simple score of birdies and bogeys posted on the first nine would convey no sense of the escalating intensity. Molinari, for example, mixed in one of each of his seven pars, but his was a fascinating tour of the opening half of the course, exemplified by the way he played the sixth. Downhill par threes are generally welcomed, but the steeply sloped green on six at Augusta National appears uninviting, as if the player were being expected to hit and hold an Alp or an Ande. Shots that fell short of the flagstick resulted in three-putts, while balls that crossed it were dead. Francesco went overboard.

If he didn't play his next one perfectly, he'd die metaphorically. A little long or short with his pitch and double bogey and a lead change would be in play, but Molinari concocted a shot that crawled up the bank on little cat's feet and a putt from about six feet that rolled at such perfect speed and path that the ball didn't touch the sides of the hole when it went in. It was his 49th hole in a row of par or better, one short of the Masters record and a couple of no-bogies ahead of Ben Hogan. His short game was excellent; his hands on a putter were flawlessly relaxed yet completely in control, similar to Federer with a tennis racquet or Clapton with a guitar. Moli was three points ahead of the rest of the field.

On seven, Tiger spun one to within a few inches for birdie three, while Francesco hooked his tee ball and ran into some pine tree trouble. He smacked his ball back into play, resulting in a brief but awkward pitch. The hill on the other side of the hole didn't aid as much as it should have, the putt from two yards didn't break as it should have, and Molinari made his first bogey since Thursday afternoon, on the eleventh hole. He'd gone 19 for 19 in making pars after missing greens.

While Francesco scrambled and recovered repeatedly, his opponent in a red shirt was engaged in an old-school shot-maker/ball-striker round a la Trevino or Hogan. Tiger appeared to be in full control, despite his driver sliding right here and a drawing left there, with conservative approaches to greens interspersed by stunning ones like the exquisite one into seven. His eerie stillness reminded those of the famous mentalist, Nicklaus. Woods would shoot a one-under-35 with birdies on seven and eight and a par on nine.

Koepka played and walked with his typical aura of invincibility, a hole ahead of the Tiger-Tony-Frankie group. The muscled safecracker lunged for every pin, ignoring all opportunity to play it safe. He also birdied the eighth, the most difficult par five at Augusta National. He went one-under on the first nine, tying Woods. The only non-major winner in the final pairing appeared unfazed, but not in the way we expected; Finau had practically vowed to wear a shirt to match the coveted jacket, but here he was in a basic white polo.

"I wear green on Sunday because it is my mother's favourite colour, but green goes with everything." "Sunday at the Masters, too," he'd remarked back when competing in the tournament was merely a pipe dream. Ravena's memory became critical following her death in an automobile accident in 2011. Tony badly missed his mum. With the pressures of his profession—he failed to qualify for the tour five times—and a wife and eventual family to support, the poor man stressed himself into a gastric ulcer back then. He couldn't walk or play golf for five weeks. So, no green shirt, but Finau did carry a talisman in his bag—or, rather, his caddie, Greg Bodine did: an Augusta National logo ball signed by 1971 champ Billy Casper, a good friend who died recently and the only Mormon to win the Masters—until now.

The wind shifted.

And the game was altered. Because there are no unattractive clicking digital scoreboards on the greens at the National, players must occasionally rely on sonar and echolocation to determine their relative positions. As in bats. People chanting very loudly in surrounding arenas marked major changes on numerous holes when none of the old hand-cranked Masters leaderboards were visible. Is that a roar from a bird or an eagle? Is that a Tiger roar or an Ian Poulter roar?

The saying "The Masters doesn't begin until the back nine on Sunday" holds enough truth to be repeated indefinitely, but if tournament and club co-founder Bobby Jones had his way, no one would ever use it. For Bobby, the terms "back side" and "back nine" were too close to a veiled reference to a human backside. That reminds me of Ned Flanders. Prissy, but that's how the Grand Slam champion rolls.

Permission to re-enter, sir? "In the inward half of the final round, the Masters begins in earnest."

Which is great because the inward half of Augusta National is the longest stretch run in sports. Better than the Churchill Downs clubhouse turn, the Iditarod's final quarter mile, and Indy's final lap, which is identical to the first lap.

Augusta National's inward half is reminiscent of nine Fenway Parks: magnificent self-contained venues, each with its own crowds, acoustics, and snack stands.

The first Fenway is the tenth hole, which has a tee shot that will make your eyelids clench. The practice green, the green and white umbrellas on the veranda, the Oak, and the clubhouse are all visible behind the player as he prepares to launch from this tee. To his left are many dazzling white, neatly groomed, black-shuttered "cottages," which is an understatement on par with describing Lake Erie as a pond. Immensity is in the foreground.

You jumped off a cliff. There's a 175-foot drop from the tee on ten to the bridge across the creek on twelve; if they get some snow this winter, we'd like to ski the ten-to-twelve run. Could they maybe include a rope tow? Something to put in the suggestion box.

But seriously, if you can swat a high hook, you're in business on ten, and you'll have an extra-long time to relish your fantastic shot, as the ball appears to float in the air for an eternity. But the golfer whose anti-hook gene prevents him from throwing a decent curveball is playing for bogey, as Tiger and Tony did in the last round. With two fantastic shots, Koepka got it up and down from the right bunker. Molinari now leads by two after a cold-blooded green-in-regulation, two-putt par.

Finau's six-foot putt for par on ten was missed, but he'd done so quickly and without resorting to the singularly irritating practice of many modern pro golfers, a pre-putt study of a topographical map. At the Masters, green maps are not permitted. Players and caddies aren't even allowed to bring their own. Thank you very much, Augusta National.

The eleventh hole is another welcoming Fenway, more snug and distinct than it used to be because of extensive evergreen planting in recent decades. Tiger bombed it right of Rush Limbaugh for the second day in a row, but for the second day in a row, he had a reasonably straightforward shot through the trees. Racing fortune.

"I was five feet away from him for that shot," local kid Ryan Gunnels remembered. "He was just chatting with Joe about numbers, but Tiger makes all the decisions." He's the most concentrated person in the room. It's almost as if he isn't human or lives on a separate planet than us."

For Ryan's friend and fellow Tiger partisan Jay Beach, seventeen, watching the man in black and red all day was equal parts war whoops and stress: "My nerves... I was quite nervous the entire day. His putts appeared to take almost twenty seconds to reach the hole." The two pals ultimately made their way up the ski hill to the eighth green to see the finish.

Molinari only missed the eleventh fairway by a few yards, but his penalty was far more than Tiger's. He had to hit his second shot low, aim it at the water hazard on the left, then spin it back to the right due to tree branches and angles. That he did. Water on ice. Sangue fresco.

What kind of stuff? You surely remember: with the Masters on the line, four of the world's finest golfers hit their dang balls in the creek from 158 yards away. Each player who used a water ball made a double bogey five on twelve.

The pin was found on the far right. The hourglass-shaped green is canted to the right, and the flagstick is a few steps further away than it appears. It was a tempting target, partially because the back bunker and the one near the water were out of bounds if you went straight for the stick. But, with so little space for a ball out there and such a hefty penalty for a miscalculation, who would be brave or reckless enough to fire right towards the yellow flag?

"Augusta babies know from the cradle that you don't shoot at the Sunday pin on twelve," said Tim Wright, a former Augusta baby.

Tim should have warned Koepka, who attacked the stick with a nine iron. Brooks' Titleist ProV1x hovered in the air like a punted football for a few seconds. Mysterious, undetected breezes overhead slightly reduced its apogee and slowed its velocity, forcing the pill to land three yards short of its target; the ball rolled backward off the lush green bank and into Rae's Creek. The audience grumbled, loud enough to be heard by the threesome heading down eleven. Was that a grunt from Koepka or a moan from Webb Simpson? Ian Poulter also lifted his wayward ball into the hazard after his obligatory spell of fretting and frowning on the twelfth tee.

"I knew it [the wind] was slightly in, and then all of a sudden it was down," Brooks later explained. "We're all aware that the wind direction changes by the second on that hole." It's all a game of chance. "Once [the ball] clears those trees..."

Tiger was observing, despite the fact that he appeared to be preoccupied with eleven.

"Joe and I had noticed that Brooksie and Poults were both in the water," Tiger explained to Henni. "I know from a lot of playing with Brooksie that he has a much stronger ball flight than I do." It cuts through the wind. And for him to fall short? "I had [that] on my list."

In addition, the ripples on the surface of the pond on eleven indicated a bit of wind from the left. Tiger deduced from this data and the washed balls of his fellow competitors that there was a headwind on twelve that could not be felt on the face or identified by tossing up grass leaves.

Missed putts and doubles for Koepka and Poulter, while Ian and Webb Simpson acted out a slow-paced drama that gave the three on the tee more time to think and worry. They have you watch Webb Simpson put in hell.

The coast was finally clear. The stream, bunkers, and green on number twelve form a simple, harmonious picture of shapes and colours. Someone who isn't literal should paint it, perhaps a Japanese landscape artist. Perhaps a modern-day Francisco Goya could bring out the awful beauty of the pit.

Moli looked up; there was no wind in the treetops, yet he knew it was there. He chose to take an extra club—an eight—but with a catch; an inch of grip protruded above his palms. He was attempting to concoct a lower shot that would be less impacted by the weird, whirling wind, but, like Brooksie and Poults, he took dead aim at the enticing pin and fell short. His Callaway ball, which had two red dots on it, crawled down the creek bank and into the water.

Embedded within the next group were sounds reflecting what was in many people's hearts: that the unexpected failure by the machine-like Moli was good for Tiger. But celebrating a mistake is not acceptable in golf, especially at the Masters, where such behaviour can result in the offending spectator being removed off the grounds by a man armed with a gun. Mr. Jones was adamant about this. Golf contrasts with tennis' questionable sportsmanship, in which opponents celebrate one another's double-faults and miss hits with a fist pump.

But if you're just reacting to the scoreboard, you may say whatever you want. The board watchers gathered around the eighteenth green screamed as one as the operator substituted Francesco's red 13 with an 11. "The crowd went crazy," Jay Beach recalled. "Everyone on 'eighteen was going insane."

Tiger's turn is at twelve o'clock. His blank expression revealed a man in full chilly mode. He aimed a nine iron thirty feet left of the stick and hooked it a touch just to be sure; the ball cleared the front bunker and stopped short of the back bunker, and the patrons roared.

Tony is now. He looked for clues about wind direction and speed, then picked a club and aimed for Tiger's ball. "I was going to hit a fade, and there was a puff of wind from the left," Finau recounted. The Utahn's ball soared even higher than Koepka's, but it was gorgeous in flight and hideous on the ground, much like a turkey vulture. It, too, landed on the lush green bank before falling into the creek. "He hit it flush, but you could just see it get killed at its peak," Tiger explained.

Tony, I wondered, why didn't you... after the other three fell short? Finau claimed that he realised he was aiming too far left in the middle of his aggressive three-quarter swing and altered microscopically to the right. To his tremendous dismay.

Daring had been beaten by cunning.

The air was thick with scepticism. The atmosphere was tense and unsettling with three of the leaders up the creek. Who was in, who was out, and, most importantly, where was Tiger?

"I was by those stands by thirteen green and fourteen tee," Dallas golf pro Gilbert Freeman recalled. "If you're in the right spot and have binoculars, you can see all the way back to the twelfth green, but not the tee." When someone—two someones—hit it in the water, we heard the disappointed murmurs. The third guy was apparently unharmed. Whoever walked up to the green first would be the safe guy. 'This is Tiger!' a couple of the binocular guys said, and the audience erupted.

"It was as if we were a collective One, all pulling in the same direction."

What a production: Tiger requested that three maintenance personnel come down their leaf blowers and clear his route to the hole after noticing three maintenance men looking from the azalea bushes and observing assorted organic schmutz in his line. They did it. Moli bogeyed from ten feet out. Tiger holed the sixth hole for a two-putt par. Finau made a double after missing from five feet. Light rain started to fall. Umbrellas opened up like azaleas in flower.

On the twelfth tee, with the adrenaline rush that only a double bogey can provide—a condition known colloquially as red ass—Koepka blasted his drive over the woods and around the curve, leaving him with only an eight-iron to the par five green.

"I wasn't deflated," Finau said a month later during his pro-am round at Colonial. "I knew I'd have eagle and birdie chances on the last six holes." But I also knew I had to perform flawlessly."

Woods referred to the current circumstance as "Pandora's box, now opened..." Now fast forward to the age of thirteen. Brooksie is an eagle maker. I create birdies. Finau hits a birdie. ... Cantlay... DJ is on a tear, and Bubba just went to ten-under in a hurry. Four men are tied for first place (at eleven under). With six holes to go, seven guys have a legitimate chance to win."

Then began the subtle game within the endgame, the process of memorising scoreboards and listening for powerful blasts of sound.

"It got very interesting trying to figure it all out," Tiger explained to Henni. He examined the leaderboard on thirteen as if it were a test. "I wanted to see where they were all, what holes they were in, just in case there were any roars." Who knows who that could be. I'm curious."

The rain stopped. The tournament was heating up.

Patrick Cantlay took the lead at -12 with an eagle on the fifteenth hole, but he was out of holes. At twelve under, Schauffele joined him. Then it was just Schauffele. Then Xander had some company. The racecars sped up to the finish line, slamming doors and trading paint. After fourteen holes, we had roughly: Woods, Molinari, and Schauffele -12.

DJ Koepka, Day, Cantlay (?) -11

Then DJ birdied seventeen, resulting in a four-way tie for first place at -12. Then Koepka's eagle putt on fifteen just missed, resulting in a five-way tie with his birdie four.

Tony and Tiger blasted long, straight drives on fifteen, both hitting the green in two with irons and would have two-putt birdies in a minute, but Moli misplayed three consecutive shots, costing him huge. He drove into the orange straw beneath the pines and was unable to go for the green in two. He chipped out too strongly, his ball racing down the fairway at the bottom of the slope and into the left rough, on rugged terrain trampled on by several fans' feet.

Patrick Reed had told us that there are three difficult shots on the inner half: the tee balls on twelve and eighteen, and this, the pitch up to the fifteenth green.

Then the worst happened: Molinari lost control of the wedge shot's height, and his ball went well up into a pine tree that wasn't in play. The Callaway ball clipped a branch and splashed into the middle of the pond. Cheers erupted when the placards on the scoreboards on seventeen and eighteen were changed—a red 13 for Tiger and the sole lead; a red 10 for Signor Francesco.

Tiger played an eight iron with a slight draw on sixteen, while Koepka watched from seventeen; it was another in a sequence of fantastic iron shots, this one a sort-of re-creation of that unbelievable slow-mo chip from 2005. The 2019 version didn't go in, but it was close, and Woods had a kick-in to go to fourteen under and a two-shot lead. He didn't?

"I hit it close on sixteen, so as I'm leaving the sixteen tee, I take one last look at the board," Tiger said Henni. 'How many men have a chance to go to fourteen—if I make par on the last two holes—if I make birdie here?'

"Like any other sport, you want to know the time and the distance."

Two more random-sounding cheers came from afar; they were the aftershocks from the scoreboard crowds reacting to Tiger's two on sixteen.

Tiger held his cool on the short walk to the seventeenth tee, while everyone else was losing theirs. His subconscious mind looked for and found relevant precedent. It was 2005 all over again: fourteen years previously, after startling the world by leaping ahead by two with his chip-in birdie on sixteen, euphoria or whatever clouded his execution and he concluded, shockingly, with two bogies and was lucky to have defeated Chris DiMarco.

The tournament director vowed never to let that happen again, and he vowed so hard with his tee ball that it appeared he could fracture the head on his M5. It was a slider, wonderfully executed and handled, and way the eff out there.

The World Number One kept firing at it from ahead. Koepka's aggressive manner complemented the occasion and revealed a lot about who he is as a competitor: Brooks is out there to win, not to finish high. Except for a so-so shot on sixteen, he struck decent to great irons on every hole on the back nine, but he had buzzard's luck with his Scotty Cameron T10 Select Newport 2 on the marble-hard greens. On thirteen, he'd made an eight-foot eagle putt, but otherwise... Lips were grazed by putts. They refused to enter. They passed by. He hit it close again on eighteen, this time from 123 yards out.

Tiger fired a strong cut at the flag from 143 yards with the same up-tempo slash he'd just used with the driver, which hit and stuck, and Our Guy was home free. Probably. He heard euphoric emanations from his gallery after a cautious two-putt, but gave no hint that he was departing his isolated concentration zone. Was he still going through time, still in 2005? He didn't say anything.

Ryan Gunnels and Jay Beach had wiggled and leapt into greenside seats by this point, finding themselves next to a willowy figure in a green jacket: former Secretary of State Condoleezza Rice. They talked. "I kinda asked her what it's like being one of the only girl members," Ryan recounted.

Woods stood behind his ball on the eighteenth tee, a three-wood in his hands, while the hyperventilating gallery fell silent. He mentally absorbed himself in the difficulty of the moment. He erased the fear inhibition. He used self-belief and discipline to his advantage. Then he swings. Hard.

The tee shot on eighteen, as Patrick Reed had mentioned, disproves the notion that Augusta National is a wide-open course, yet Tiger's low, blasted slider kept inside the tunnel of trees. The ball, though, rolled right, leaving a tough second shot that would become pretty damn difficult if Koepka made his eight-foot putt for birdie to move within one.

One problem with remembering the following few minutes—or all of the minutes in the 2019 Masters—is that the reader already knows how the drama ended. But nothing was predetermined at the moment. Koepka had another birdie putt within ten feet, and making it would change everything.

Brooks was debriefed a few minutes later by CBS-TV reporter Amanda Balionis. Tell us about the age of eighteen, she said.

"Don't know if I can say it on the air," Golf Yoda answered. He'd made a good putt. The ball did not go in.

Now, a bogey five would give Tiger a one-shot victory over Brooks, Xander, and DJ. The wise decision would be to use all five shots. He did. Tiger aimed way left from the right edge of the fairway, with tree limbs in his path and 169 yards to the hole, and spun the ball back to the right. He'd wisely left a forty-yard third that would avoid any pits of bright white powdered quartz. This was remarkably similar to how Hogan played the hole when he won with a bogey in 1951.

In contrast, in a similar situation in 1961, tournament leader Arnold Palmer shook patrons' hands and accepted pats on the back as he headed up the ultimate fairway—only to lose by one after scoring a double bogey. That would not be Tiger's fate; he kept his game face on and, except from pulling his hat off briefly, he did not acknowledge the cheers. Billy Kratzert delivered more of his trademark verbless statements on television. "The determination to return," he explained. "To be able to have this opportunity."

Tiger made a two-putt from ten feet. He'd won again two years after back troubles nearly paralyzed him, a decade after a heartbreaking domestic scandal, eleven years since his last major, and fourteen years since his last first in the Masters. He flung back his head and shouted. All hell had broken loose.

Tiger hugged Tony, shook hands with Tony's caddie, Moli and Moli's caddie, and then joyfully hugged the group's third devoted looper, Joe LaCava. Then came the embraces of his son, mother, daughter, and girlfriend, all of whom had returned from the war. There were four more roaring embraces with other close friends, then a big one for Steinie.

Suddenly, there is chanting! "Ti-ger, Ti-ger, Ti-ger"—ten reps, and a few more afterwards; it was an honour never granted even to the greatest Masters heroes, Jack and Arnie, though it should be noted that people chant more now than they used to.

The new champ led the way uphill to the clubhouse as if he were a speedboat and his mother, children, and girlfriend were attached water skiers. Fans were ecstatic to get a hug from the old/new Master.

Some of his brother's golf pros were waiting for him outside the scoring area. Trevor Immelman, Zach Johnson, Ricky Fowler, Justin Thomas, Bubba Watson, Ian Poulter, Xander Schauffele, and Bernhard Langer all smiled and grabbed Tiger's right hand. The first among equals, Koepka, then stood apart from the others. They exchanged hugs.

"You finish second place, you're a little bummed out," Brooks later told the press, but he wasn't this time, and he knew he wasn't alone. "There was a monsoon of people after he won there on eighteen." It's amazing."

A monsoon of people.

Jim Nantz said, "The completion of one of the great comebacks in any sport, all-time," as TV showed replays of Tiger embracing Earl and Tiger with armfuls of his own kids just now, and then Jim and Tiger were hustling to the Butler Cabin studio for part one of the Presentation of the Threads. Part two of the green jacket event was the actual deal, with people being acknowledged and speeches being given. Following the brief television interlude, it would take place on the putting green.

Francesco was approached by Ms. Balionis. "I think I made a few new fans today with those two double bogies," he reflected, a rueful smile on his face. "On twelve, it was just a bad swing." I simply made a mess at fifteen.

"I'm proud of how calm I remained even after making blunders... On the back nine, I was a little less aggressive and lost focus a little bit, which is strange to say in these conditions, but it's been a long week and it's not easy to hit every shot one hundred percent."

The man who seemed to hit every shot perfectly had taken a seat in the cool cellar of the Butler Cabin. Chairman Ridley and Nantz were sitting across from him. Patrick Reed sat on his left, wearing a green jacket and carrying another. Viktor Hovland, the competition's low amateur, was to his right. When it was his turn to speak, the cheerful young man from Oslo credited his Oklahoma State University golf coach, Alan Bratton, who had caddied for him.

In answer to Nantz, Tiger attempted to explain how and why he'd had roughly one shot's worth of mental endurance over the others. He'd stayed present and focused, as well as in control of his emotions, he claimed, but basically he was "just plodding my way around the golf course all day, just plodding my way around." "All of a sudden, I had the lead," a fitting reference to the Immortal Meltdown on Twelve.

In sports, there is a call and response tradition in which a reporter asks the new champ, "Has it sunk in yet?" and the new champ is almost always expected to say "no." Nantz didn't bother, but Henni and Tiger acknowledged the ritual in their very first exchange. But, in my opinion, diving in isn't worth it. Sinking in and staring at the fire are reserved for retirement years. Sinking in refers to the jeweller's chisel being used on the prize. Perhaps Tiger should focus as much as possible on the 2019 Masters in order to keep his wonderful lucky comeback win fresh in his thoughts for as long as possible, rather than simply filling it away. For if there was ever a time to relish, this was it.

"To have my kids there," Tiger stated to Fred, Jim, Viktor, Patrick, and the millions of people watching from home. "It's all come full circle now." My father visited in 1997. Now I'm the father."

Reed stood up, Tiger stood up, and the rest took a step back. The defending champion held out the jacket, and the new champion discovered the arm holes.

"It fits!" exclaimed Tiger.

The contents of this book may not be copied, reproduced or transmitted without the express written permission of the author or publisher. Under no circumstances will the publisher or author be responsible or liable for any damages, compensation or monetary loss arising from the information contained in this book, whether directly or indirectly. .

Disclaimer Notice:

Although the author and publisher have made every effort to ensure the accuracy and completeness of the content, they do not, however, make any representations or warranties as to the accuracy, completeness, or reliability of the content. , suitability or availability of the information, products, services or related graphics contained in the book for any purpose. Readers are solely responsible for their use of the information contained in this book

Every effort has been made to make this book possible. If any omission or error has occurred unintentionally, the author and publisher will be happy to acknowledge it in upcoming versions.

Printed in Great Britain
by Amazon

31495770R00069